URBAN ECOLOGY

McGRAW-HILL SERIES IN
POPULATION BIOLOGY

Consulting Editors
Paul R. Ehrlich, Stanford University
Richard W. Holm, Stanford University

BRIGGS: Marine Zoogeography
EDMUNDS and LETEY: Environmental Administration
EHRLICH, HOLM, and PARNELL: The Process of Evolution
GEORGE and McKINLEY: Urban Ecology: In Search of an Asphalt Rose
HAMILTON: Life's Color Code
POOLE: An Introduction to Quantitative Ecology
STAHL: Vertebrate History: Problems in Evolution
WATT: Ecology and Resource Management
WATT: Principles of Environmental Science
WELLER: The Course of Evolution

URBAN ECOLOGY

In Search of an Asphalt Rose

CARL J. GEORGE
Associate Professor of
Biological Sciences
Union College

DANIEL McKINLEY
Associate Professor of
Biological Sciences
State University
of New York at Albany

McGRAW-HILL BOOK COMPANY

New York St. Louis San Francisco Düsseldorf
Johannesburg Kuala Lumpur London Mexico
Montreal New Delhi Panama Paris São Paulo
Singapore Sydney Tokyo Toronto

Library of Congress Cataloging in Publication Data

George, Carl J
Urban ecology: in search of an asphalt rose.

(McGraw-Hill series in population biology)
Includes bibliographical references.
1. Sociology, Urban. 2. Human ecology.
I. McKinley, Daniel, joint author. II. Title.
[DNLM: 1. Ecology. QH541 G347u 1974]
HT151.G37 301.31 74-814
ISBN 0-07-023087-0
ISBN 0-07-023086-2 (pbk.)

URBAN ECOLOGY
In Search of an Asphalt Rose

1234567890BABA7987654

This book was set in Times Roman by Black Dot, Inc. The editors were William J. Willey and Barry Benjamin; the designer was Joseph Gillians; the production supervisor was Thomas J. LoPinto. George Banta Company, Inc., was printer and binder.

To
Gail George
and
Margaret McKinley

Contents

Preface

Apart from the satisfaction of putting things down on paper, this book was written for the student of cities. It is a blended or straddling book (depending upon your disciplinary addictions) drawing from many of the customary viewpoints, and for this reason, we can almost guarantee that it will evoke strong response. We believe it to be good seasoning—i.e., as an ancillary text—for the more traditional introductory courses of urban planning, economics, sociology, political science, ecology, geography, and resource conservation. The book should also stand as the primary text in shorter undergraduate courses dealing with urban ecology, urban studies, and human ecology. With the use of the lengthy bibliography, it should prove a fine device for generating discussion and follow-up.

For the pedagogue who has tunnel vision, it will prove little short of anathema. We have already sensed this from the previews which have been solicited by the several editors who have worked with us. We would only ask that staunch disciplinarians consider whence cometh their strong response and whether the work might thus provoke useful debate in the classroom.

The message of the book is that as most cities are now constructed, they are bad places for human beings and other kinds of living things to be. We sense that, given the growing pressures of resource shortages, they will become progressively worse. They are bad because their peoples have broken away from their foundations in terms of both awareness of what and where their primal resources are. We believe this estrangement has reached disastrous proportions and scream with loud numbers and petulant subjectivity toward this end. If the reader is an urbanite of several generations he may not, unfortunately, sense this estrangement or its implications, but he usually will evidence it in the character of his actions. Sadly, many of these ecological illiterates are in positions of great administrative power and influence.

As a solution we urge the return of living diversity to urban areas. We believe that this process can and will be a major focus for a new breed of engineering, architectural, and urban design. We think school locations, with their architecture and the use of surrounding lands, are good places to begin. We would also like to see the emergence of a new private, accredited professional—the land doctor—who will serve to improve the health of a battered earth and preserve that of the more intact remaining wild places.

We endorse the preservation of our magnificent national and state parklands, but we feel that these parks are distant pieces of pie in the sky for many Americans. We think that the real environment, where we spend most of our lives, is in the shadow of orthagonal office buildings and bleak, gray factories. These are the places which almost totally obscure the realization of true human potential. We need to give more attention to the creation of the natural city, a place where food, plants, and humans may grow up side by side and where human wastes are used productively rather than be abused and discarded, as is now the case.

We do not give great detail to population explosion or

various technical disasters. These are treated well elsewhere. The two-headed beast of too many people and too many untested innovations is certainly a major problem. We affirm this. In this book we have accented another key problem—the importance of restoring the city to health through the bringing back of the *others*, those organisms with which we truly must share this one planet upon which we find ourselves.

Our appreciation is extended to our editors for their assistance in attaining this goal.

Carl J. George
Daniel McKinley

URBAN ECOLOGY

Part One

Definitions and Perspectives

A complete way of life for man presupposes unrestricted access to the countryside as well as the town, to soil as well as to pavement, to flora and fauna as well as to libraries and theaters. A balanced way of life presupposes a lasting equilibrium between land and city; animals, men, and plants; air, water, and industry.

Lewis Herber
Our Synthetic Environment

Land, then is not merely soil; it is a fountain of energy flowing through a circuit of soils, plants, and animals. . . . The velocity and character of the upward flow of energy depend on the complex structure of the plant and animal community. . . .

When a change occurs in one part of the circuit, many other parts must adjust themselves to it. . . . Evolutionary changes, however, are usually slow and local. Man's invention of tools has enabled him to make changes of unprecedented violence, rapidity, and scope.

Aldo Leopold
A Sand County Almanac

Chapter 1

The City Defined

Census figures show that the central city, with its aggregated buildings and crowded people, is being abandoned. Even so, explosive pressures in the city still exist. Between 1950 and 1960, America's total population grew by 19 percent but the population of big-city metropolitan areas increased by 27 percent. Between 1960 and 1970 the growth rate in metropolitan areas was 13 percent, compared to 11 percent for the country as a whole. Two facts about the growth of big American cities within recent years are shocking. First, while the suburban rings have been inflated by 25 percent, the so-called "central cities" have actually declined by 0.5 percent. Second, there has been a drastic reorganization of city centers along racial lines. While the white population in the cities dropped by 2.1 million in the 1960s, black numbers grew by 2.6 million.

But the apartheid does not stop with blacks (and other nonwhite groups) living apart from whites. The segregated races gather in turn in ethnic clans, and these separate further into classes.

A different kind of separation results because the specialists of the system tend to remain in distinct groups: lawyers spend their most functional hours with other lawyers; engineers work with other engineers; and so on and on. Segregation by age also occurs. The young are collected in schools, the old go to senior citizen centers, and the "productive" (in tax terms) age groups form their own series of divisions.

Of all the apartnesses which mark our day, however, it is the apartness from wilderness which plays the most important role in creating and shaping the anxieties so typical of our culture. Water no longer comes from a spring or stream, but from the metal of a faucet, metal seemingly unrelated to a distant watershed in the Adirondacks. Eggs appear in plastic containers on supermarket shelves. Their relationship to chickens, let alone the sources of chicken-feed protein in the fish of the cold waters off the west coast of South America, is rarely considered. When we have finished with these products of distant places, we throw them into our sinks and sewers as if we were committing them to oblivion. The severely overtaxed landfill sites, the murky lifeless waters, the wind-drifted papers (even if only on the lot next door) seem unrelated, a part of another world. Thus we experience the estrangement of men from resources.

When men grow so apart from the sources of real wealth and from one another, there grows a deep and sullen anxiety. Unlike organized violence it is not the subject of daily, conscious thought and conversation. It is the substance of a quiet terror that drives men into the acts of cruelty, violence, and malignant behavior that so mark our cities today. It is this estrangement, this inability to participate in coherent social processes, which marks the modern American urbanite. It is his dedication to segmentalism and to blind specialization that sets his type apart. It is not simply that he lives in a certain place on the surface of the Earth. The lakeside resident an hour's drive from the nearest population center may still be an urbanite. Conversely, a dweller in a city may not be an urbanite, although, if he is not, the odds are good that the city will not serve him well.

Let us try to define "suburbanization." Moving to the suburbs is often a futile process of changing one's place in space without changing one's mind. The affluent urbanite feels the alienation resulting from his separateness, and responds to a new mythology of nature created by our arts and mass media. He vainly searches for the "natural" ideal portrayed in the cigarette ad showing a lovely couple beside an unspoiled stream. He yearns for the automobile adman's fantasy: the same couple just alighted from their car, which stands, trackless, beside untouched ocean sands. His search leads him to move to the countryside—along with all his friends. But he remains hooked on, or hooked into, his specialty and bound into his own belief structure of how things work.

But what is meant by the word "natural," as it will be used in the pages ahead? In a fuller sense all events, substances, and structures are natural. The Empire State Building is no less natural than a skein of Canada geese flying northward for the summer. An untended dump site filled with abandoned cars, refrigerators, and sodden mattresses riddled by rats is no less natural than a forest glen filled with the song of spring birds. All is nature. The real point, however, is that one set of "natural" conditions may be conducive to survival; the other may not. Since man is part of the whole of nature, it behooves him to decide effectively where his priorities lie and to act accordingly.

Somehow, we have come to accept "natural" to mean the ecologically good and "unnatural" the ecologically evil. The difficulty, of course, is that we are not yet, and perhaps may never be, clever enough to predict reliably the consequences of our actions. It may take us centuries or longer to evaluate the acts of some of our present-day creative citizens. Knowledge of good and evil comes only through prolonged interaction of all parts of the whole and only when the human citizen is in contact with other biotic citizens, most of whom reside outside of the city.

We avoid such expressions as "man versus nature" and "man apart from nature." Instead, we shall talk of "wilderness," that set of circumstances where man participates as a responsible citizen in a biotic community, not as a "master" or "steward."

Unfortunately, we find very little wilderness about us today.

A wilderness resident lives close to the sources of his well-being—to water, to food, and to other essential substances. He understands them in a very basic way and respects them. The usual commercial farmer does not live in the wilderness, of course, but he is closer to essential understanding than most of us.

Travel and camping are, like the flight to suburbia, attempts to escape the pressures of urban life by a return to nature. Two and a half million camping vehicles spending 45 million nights in American parks do not guarantee a return to nature. People try. The result has been abandonment of parts of many cities as architectural graveyards. For all the efforts of their city fathers, Detroit, Pittsburgh, Albany, Buffalo, St. Louis, New Orleans, Baltimore, and Philadelphia are but a few of the cities with lifeless or moribund central areas. One may see in any city with a population greater than 1 million the gray cankers of the disease. Smaller urban areas survive where some healthier ratio of wilderness to architected city exists, but the infection often seems already transmitted.

But cities do not die alone. They turn gray much that is around them. The expansion of suburbia destroys topsoil, ruins watersheds, impairs water quality, squeezes out agriculture, clashes with forest production, assaults pests with chemicals whose effects linger on and on. The blind feeding upon distant resources becomes more and more parasitic.

The traditional city as magnet is no longer holding society together. The ecology of the nonurban landscape, the primal environment that gave us birth and nurture, is cracking up. Just where do we, as urban people stand? What can we, for our own good, do?

Chapter 2

Ecology in Perspective

Ecology has become a magic word, a "science" the proper study of which is supposed to cure all ills. In a certain way, when used in connection with urbanism, the word "ecology" has returned to its roots. The Greek word *oikos* meant dwelling place, house, perhaps particularly the sacred hearth of a house. Oecology, as it used to be spelled, is thus the study of the essence of the household. Perhaps there *is* magic in the idea that the whole Earth is man's sacred household.

Oikos is also found in the Greek compound *oikonomos,* "a steward," where *nomos* means "to distribute." This implies household management, hence our modern word economy. How sad that economy and ecology, with beginnings so similar, seem to have wandered so far apart in our day!

For a long time, ecologists studied nature as far as possible from human disturbances. They were not simply avoiding stepping on the toes of other professionals, such as economists and sociologists. They were looking to wilderness areas, relatively undisturbed by man, for basic information that only nature apart from man can give. Their studies have been fruitful. Although the urgent need to explore wilderness in salt marsh, bog, alpine tundra, forest, and grassland continues, it is now time for ecologists to return to the city.

Ecology in its present sense was first used by the German zoologist Ernst Haeckel in 1869 and he meant it to apply to relationships between the environment and an organism's heredity. The modern emphasis is upon interaction, upon process.

The interactions with which ecologists concern themselves are interactions of living and nonliving things as in rain to mountain, ant to soil, and ant to ant lion. Interactions always work both ways, even among nonliving elements. A mountain causes rain to fall and rainfall in turn erodes the mountain to a plain. Plants occupy mountain soil and the nature of mountain soil is changed. Plants change erosion rates and they conserve nutrients and enhance rates of soil formation. Vegetation may cause the character of rainfall to alter both on the mountain and in areas under the mountain's influence. Man builds a city and in a multitude of ways molds the landscape. But the new landscape molds man. All this is ecology.

Cities bring many ecological changes. For example, the average temperature in cities becomes warmer than in suburban or rural areas, and either more or less rain may fall. Good or bad? Some people object to being warmer by several degrees in summer than their country cousins. Others may like the saving in fuel that a few degrees of warmth makes possible; but they may not like the increased fog that such conditions tend to bring. Areas in the lee of major conurbations, such as Chicago and Buffalo, now receive more precipitation than they did several decades ago and this precipitation often falls in torrential amounts. How do you decide whether this is good or bad? Some aspects of air pollution offer another example of good-and-bad. Industrial and automotive activities increase ozone (O_3, a form of the oxygen molecule), which has germ-killing powers. So far, so good, perhaps. But, aside from the fact that ozone can be toxic for man if concentrations are high enough, ozone also absorbs ultraviolet light. Since the latter is also a germ killer, we do not know how the balance lies.

VISUALIZING ECOLOGY

Ecological processes can be understood to have originated in three steps: the appearance of Earth as a *stage*, the provision of the stage with *actors*, and the *play* that then resulted.

All science is an exercise in description, and the description of Earth as a stage is fairly straightforward, taking many of its descriptive terms directly from the sciences of geology, astronomy, physics, chemistry, paleontology, and meteorology. This is the abiotic or nonliving world and it is divided into *place* and *platform*.

Place

Where you are on this globe of ours, in terms of latitude and longitude, determines the distribution of the sun's energy and the amount of it that you can share in. Rays of the sun beam straight down upon the tropics and bring out a riot of life; at least they do if the energy is tamed by abundant rain. The glancing rays of light that strike the north pole (and the south pole six months later, for summer alternates at the poles) deliver less heat per square mile of surface. The poles are not only cold. Less food is produced per year, and fewer species of organisms have evolved. Biotic conditions are simpler and climatic conditions in general harsher as you go poleward from the tropics.

Platform

Underfoot is the geological platform. It may be made up of granites or other crystalline rocks. Or rocks may be metamorphic (changed by pressure, chemicals, or heat) or sedimentary (such as sandstone, limestone, and shale). Different soils develop from different rocks. Rocks, whatever their variety, may be thrust up into mountains, laterally shifted as mobile continental masses, or folded into valleys. The hardness and solubility of rocks and the angles at which they lie influence both surface features and the nature of soil.

Both place and platform also interact to modify and mold atmospheric conditions that give a particular area its weather. The long-term interplay of all such conditions produces climate. From the intertwining of climate, place, and platform emerge such major aspects of geography as rivers, lakes, and estuaries, as well as the particular smaller influences such as pH (a measure of acidity and alkalinity), mineral content, depth, and temperatures. For these reasons, rivers and lakes differ considerably in different parts of the world.

This complex system of interacting chemical processes and physical structures and systems occurs as a whirlpool flow of events. Yet it has great permanency. The abiotic stage, more complex than any arena yet built by man, challenges the adaptive capacities of all living things.

A relatively complete and reliable description of the abiotic stage is, thus, not simple. Describing the biotic responses—the evolutionary matter of providing the stage with *actors*—is even more complicated. These biotic responses, made during more than 2 billion years of time in the form of several million species of living things, are life's answers to the diversity of habitats available. That is to say, not all answers can be found by studying the organisms themselves. Since the day of Charles Darwin, we have come to think of organisms as being "adapted." But adapted to what? Actors fit the stage they act upon, so part of the answer lies within the physical habitats of organisms.

Ecology is, of course, much more complex than this suggests. For example, there is the time factor. The "unchanging" mountains change radically over geological time, and, with organisms present, old habitats are forever altering and new lifeways (or *niches,* as they are called) being created. Consider a tree that invades a floodplain where only grass grew before. The tree's living or dead trunk, leaves, twigs, flowers, fruits, and seeds each support unique species of insects. Trees shade the soil, modify temperature and moisture, and change the character of the soil. Humidity increases in the air near the Earth, where most organisms live. Freshwater runoff may be almost entirely eliminated.

Snow is trapped in winter, either in the canopy or on the shaded ground where it melts slowly. Action and reaction occur everywhere and in all directions.

This is the *play,* the interaction among actors upon the stage. This play, in both the pool of events within natural communities today and in the long perspective of geological time, represents the great transactions among nonlife and life, and life and life.

But too much is going on for us to talk very long of ecology simply in terms of shapes and species and structures. The transaction of the ecological play is divided into two parts, a dance of energy and materials in the actors themselves and the guiding activities of the regulators.

The dance includes all biological-chemical-physical processes and machinery and is commonly called the *ecosystem* (short for ecological system).

All energy is derived from transformations of atoms. Events in the nuclei of atoms in the sun shower us with solar radiant energy. We are burned by it or warmed by it, but only our sister organisms, the living photosynthetic plants and bacteria, can grasp and store it in chemical bonds. We are entirely dependent upon them or, less directly, upon certain of their consumers which we kill and use as food. The current irrational (irrational because of its blindness to the future) exploitation of fossil fuels such as coal and petroleum merely taps a stored product of solar radiation of plants that lived and died long ago.

No organic activity occurs without expenditure or input of energy. The most commonplace events as well as the most complex and unusual ones are all faces of the mysterious process of energy transformation. But we are not, in conventional terms anyway, bundles of energy. We are constellations of atoms of carbon, hydrogen, oxygen, nitrogen, and much else—constellations that walk, run, swim, soar, and think when properly fired with proper amounts of the sun's nuclear energy.

But this momentary or sustained influence of energy upon matter is only part of the story. If solar energy is not fixed in chemical bonds, it enters Earth's orbit only long enough to go through one or a few changes. It then passes off into the heat sink of nearly empty space. Even energy bound in various molecules, unless fossilized, rarely stays as chemical bond energy for long. Energy is in flux. That is, it flows.

In contrast to energy, matter, in the form of atoms and molecules, is mostly a stay-at-home. Materials, particularly those identified with living systems, all *cycle,* that is, they may be used again and again. For example, carbon atoms go from the air into a plant leaf. They become parts of a carbohydrate molecule and the plant leaf is eaten by an animal. The carbon atom then goes from a plant eater to an animal eater. Many steps in a complicated dance may take place before the carbon atom is finally deprived of its chemical bond energy and turned back to the atmosphere.

The above is a description of a cycle known as the carbon cycle. Different cycles occur with nitrogen, phosphorus, and other atoms.

Energy-bearing molecules move together through ecosystems. Their movements can be described and calculated at three levels of complexity: *food chain, food web, and food pyramid.*

A food chain may begin when sunlight and carbon dioxide are joined by a one-celled photosynthetic alga in the sea. This microscopic plant is eaten by a tiny shrimp, which is then harvested by a larger shrimp. The energy-bearing molecule of carbohydrate may, of course, be oxidized (that is, "burned" and its energy released) anywhere along the line so far described. But suppose it goes on to a whale, thence to a Norwegian fisherman, and finally to bacteria of decay when the fisherman dies. Alternatively, it might go from a shrimp, to a small fish such as sardine, to a herring, to a giant tuna. The tuna may rot as a fisherman's trophy, or it may be fetched to the mainland and become small lumps of meat among vegetables and goo in tunafish salad.

The interactions between the various links of a food chain tend, in evolution, to become more and more specialized and hence more efficient. Better strategies for escape are matched by more sophisticated mechanisms of capture. Energy and materials are used more and more efficiently. The individual who survives lives on and, in a very real sense, tells his children about it. In successful encounters, both giving and receiving links of the chain profit from the emerging constraints. As the predatory forms of one interaction become the prey of another, a series of mutual adaptations can be discerned. The efficacy of these interactions in the forging of ecological hardware can be appreciated if you look at the lion's teeth or the antelope's trim form.

But food-chain interactions are never quite so simple. What happens if a single link in a particularly specialized chain breaks? The prey loses its constraints; the predator goes hungry or perhaps even becomes extinct. Thus specialization can leave both prey and predator with a shortage of alternatives. The "answer" for the ecosystem is to provide alternatives. A predator may have several possible prey species; prey species then have several forms of constraint.

The interconnected net of relationships that emerges is what ecologists call a food web, which involves far more than just the conduction of energy and materials along chains. Since it adds stability and resiliency to the whole ecosystem, it helps to balance the loss of efficiency that may occur when specialization is sacrificed in order to allow alternatives.

Three kinds of links are built into ecological food webs. There are the *primary producers,* which capture energy from sunlight. There are *primary consumers,* which harvest the producers, and secondary consumers (etc.), which harvest the primary consumers. Thus the webs appear to pyramid into a few top predatory forms, usually few in numbers and large in size. *Decomposers* make up the third category of feeders. They are the bacteria and fungi, and they feed upon leftovers from the other sorts of organisms in the community and then utilize the bodies of those organisms when they die. They convert it all back (minus the energy) into the essential nutrients of new generations of producer cells. Thus the cycle of matter in the ecosystem depends upon the ecological trinity of producers, consumers, and decomposers. Interestingly enough, the tiniest of living things sit at the top of all biotic pyramids. No participant in life's banquet can hope long to escape their attentions, or live very long without the help of their activities.

HOW LIFE RUNS ITSELF

What are the processes that give stability to the self-sustaining whirlpool of energy and matter that we call an ecosystem? Who are the directors of our ecological play, wherein form and pattern (that is, equilibrium) result from the substance and sustenance that are being continuously fluxed through the dance?

We have already spoken of the biotic pyramid. This so-called pyramidal relationship can be visualized. If you somehow calculate the weight of the living material produced by plants in a forest in a year, you have a food or trophic level, which may be labeled level 1. You will find that it weighs more than all the living matter that is produced per year by the herbivorous animals (such as grasshoppers and mice) that eat only plant material. Thus, these plant eaters make up a smaller body of living material, in this case flesh, food level 2. Now weigh the amount of flesh produced by animals living directly upon these plant-eating animals (the primary carnivores, which may include such animals as weasels, small owls, and songbirds). Their bulk, which makes up food level 3, will be less than that in level 2. And so on, right up to the top, with the top level being in general occupied by those large and conspicuous creatures that we mentioned above, as well as by those tiny and abundant creatures called decomposers.

There is little mystery about the shape of the biotic pyramid. It reflects the fact that no level can turn the matter of the level upon which it lives into its own flesh with 100 percent efficiency. In fact, the efficiency of conversion is likely to be about 10 percent for grass into herbivore, and somewhat more, but certainly nothing like 100 percent, for meat eaters. Thus there is less and less weight of flesh produced per unit of time as you go up the pyramid.

Thus we customarily think of predator-prey relationships as parts of a regulatory system, whether we talk of plants and grazing mammals or field mice and hawks. Matters are more complex than we think and there is much to be learned. Clearly, however, there are changing and yet stable relationships among predatory forms and their prey.

Another regulatory tendency found in ecosystems is that habitat-destroying forms in nature often help to displace themselves. Many ecologists discern a relationship between poorly protective, badly integrated species and disturbed and unstable areas such as eroded slopes, mud-covered river banks, plowed fields, burned areas, and deforested regions that lose nutrients rapidly. The pioneer organisms, as they are called, actually thrive upon instability. Fortunately, either because of their own actions or because of changes brought about by associated species, pioneers are usually replaced by more stable, nutrient-conserving members in an ecosystem. The whole process, ending in a relatively self-sustaining system, is called *ecological succession* (or secondary succession, since most such repair is in areas that were previously vegetated). Replacement and adjustment come about due to differences in both inherited demands and in competitive ability among the organisms of the ecosystem.

Energy, too, is a regulator. This is as true of a short-lived whirlpool in a stream as it is of a sustained and complex ecosystem, whether the latter is on a mountainside or in a wheat field. Both whirlpool and ecosystem "go" because of a relatively constant input of energy. Energy, in both cases, ends up as heat and is dispersed. Matter, in both cases, is constantly used, circulated, stored, and recycled.

A final key to regulation must be sought in the nature of biotic organization itself. A match flares up and burns itself out within a short time. The gigantic vortex of air called a tornado rushes rapidly to its own destruction. A forest ecosystem may last centuries or millenia. Differences among these systems are due to the amounts and qualities of "information" they contain. *Information* is whatever, when coupled with a "reading process," makes possible the creation of order and wise choices among alternatives. The transmission and processing of information is an old story in evolution and ecology, and information joins energy and materials to become the third component of the ecosystem. Man's ability to utilize information is merely an extension of tendencies that have always been present in the biotic world.

We have little trouble predicting the behavior of systems with lesser information content, for example, the atoms in a gas or the molecules of the lighted match. But not only do large organic molecules have more independence from the endless buffetings that atoms and small molecules are liable to, but some of them also have much more information. Because of that, they are able to make "decisions" regarding the structuring of their immediate environments.

Molecules are organized into cells; cells are organized into tissues and organs. There is a very special sharpening of cellular abilities in the division of labor that provides brain cells in some parts of an organ system and muscle cells in another. This is the way up the ladder of increased capacity for information storage and processing. Even though each step is firmly based upon the one below, each new step is a magnitude removed from the one below it in capability for new activities.

The individual organism thus emerges, a competing and cooperating entity of informed and energetic substance. It has the capacity to modify environment and to soften habitat. It can respond to its surroundings: in the short term by individual adjustment, in the long run by evolutionary genetic change. It regulates the acidity and composition of its own blood and body fluids. It maintains in many cases a remarkably constant internal temperature. It uses many strategies to make the best choices among the various alternatives offered by complexly fluctuating external conditions. Consider what a triumph this organism is, when compared to an atom, in its independence from raw natural forces both great and small and in its powers for innovative actions!

You know how chromosomes carry information from the original fertilized egg into every new cell of your body. In the study of heredity, you learn to account for the information that plants and animals have in their chromosomes and for its transmission from generation to generation. What about the ability of ecosystems to survive the broad array of pressures and disasters to which they are submitted? Think of fire, wind, drought, pest infestations, and all the rest. Obviously, the information about all this resides in the organisms that make up the ecosystem. These organisms are guided by cues offered by the total environment, which includes other organisms. We can predict, therefore, that the more species there are in an ecosystem, the more information is there, and the greater the system's stability and capacity to recover from disturbances.

It is obvious that, as we go from individual organisms to the ecosystem, we have ascended a rung of the information ladder. All higher animals are the roducts of genetic action; however, their central nervous systems are able to deal with information at still another level, in terms of both quality and amount.

To all other steps up the information ladder, man has added language and literature, and in modern technical systems, universities, and libraries, he has utilized extensive means to store and process information on this level. Thus man has extended his competitive base from pole to pole, from the ocean's depths into space, and, in the process, has displaced many other organisms. But, as already pointed out, many ecosystem functions are not being carried on by man (how can man possibly know how to run an ecosystem?). Others are being further upset. Many basic human needs are being denied or overlooked. We may well ask what future we can reasonably predict for this human-intellectual tornado.

AN EPILOGUE TO ECOLOGY AND ENERGY

Surely, if it is to serve us, our swirl of energy-matter-information must be formed into a dynamic equilibrium. A dynamism that knows no bounds tears itself apart.

But to what end shall we dedicate our species' hurricane? Briefly, we suggest that the special role of man is to contribute self-awareness to the universe—to fulfill our potential in conformity with universal forces. Obviously, man alive or dead cannot disobey any of the laws of the universe. A hard look at the ecosystem, however, will show that natural morality is not just whatever you can get away with in the short run. We believe that there are organic laws and that they are being broken by man today. The rest of this book discusses how we can work up to a better understanding of man in nature. We think this will occur when we displace the old morality that sees man as master, man as having dominion. Our seeking for a new morality must include full understanding and a will to live in harmony rather than in destructiveness.

It is probable that we must begin to see ecological truths as being of a senior order in comparison to the cultural truths that we have long lived by. This is not meant to disparage the latter. It merely means that cultures, as they achieve greater control of information, do not always know what to do with it. Cultural "truths" are ancient and intuitive and serve many and often devious motives. Ecological truths are as immediate as a burn, and as eternal as now. They are not static or doctrinaire, and they are productive of ever-changing results. They are open to human rationality. Although they are not tender toward feelings, prejudices, and emotions, they are not vindictively opposed to them either.

Civilization, for all its marvels, is a collection of cultural, social, environmental, and genetic entities that are forever in danger of being out of date. Our societies and cultures have worked not only yesterday but also a thousand or more years ago. But for some of us, tomorrow will be so different that we cannot survive. The environments that we seem to be creating for ourselves today differ more and more from the environments to which we have been beautifully adapted over the centuries. Ecological truths will frequently be hard to understand, even though we sometimes have the power, as now, to alter them. We can easily fail to use such power wisely unless we appeal to the combined information pooled in the genes of all species of organisms known to us and in all existing human cultures.

Part Two

The Gathering of the Clan

The loves we share with a city are often secret loves. Old walled towns like Paris, Prague, and even Florence are closed in on themselves and hence limit the world that belongs to them. But Algiers (together with certain other privileged places such as cities on the sea) opens to the sky like a mouth or a wound. In Algiers one loves the commonplaces: the sea at the end of every street, a certain volume of sunlight, the beauty of the race. And, as always, in that unashamed offering there is a secret fragrance. In Paris it is possible to be homesick for space and a beating of wings. Here at least man is gratified in every wish and, sure of his desire, can at last measure his possessions.

Albert Camus
"Summer in Algiers" in The Myth of Sisyphus and Other Essays

It should be obvious then why every elite has emerged from and has remained associated with the town community. The countryside is hardly the place for the development of those arts which, as Xenophon said, are sustained by agriculture. The progress of these arts requires the commercial and intellectual intercourse that only a busy place such as the town can provide. The power-motive of society—to use one of Marx's expressions—thus concentrated into town has never since ceased to maintain from there a firm hold on the rural community in spite of being tributary to it for means of biological existence.

Nicholas Georgescu-Roegen
The Entropy Law and the Economic Process

Chapter 3

First Steps

Regardless of how anything as outlandish as man evolved in the first place, we find likely ancestors of ours associated with the tree-sprinkled savannas of Africa. The time was the great, unstable period of the Pleistocene, which began perhaps 2 million years ago. With ice ages cooling certain lands and drying out others, it was a trying time to be alive. Certain lower-latitude forests, for example, became discontinuous and clumpy, with stretches of grassland between clumps. Some of our nearer ancestors survived by becoming adapted to life on the ground, away from forests.

The broad savannas required alertness, intelligence, and sociality for survival. As a social being, man was able to capitalize upon the rich landscape of the grassy plains—to ensure not just survival but really affluent survival, based upon rich animal protein. It was probably his life as social hunter that did much to mold the man we now know. Populations seized upon such evolutionary advances in bodily equipment as increased intelligence and size, and the ability to walk more erect. Groupings, pairing, parental care, and language enlarged cultural horizons.

Beginnings were simple. There is little to hint when the first tool was used. Nor can we guess with assurance when the first tool was used to make other tools, a really distinct advance for mankind. Fire was long ago taken advantage of, even when not actually made at will. Men harvested fleeing animals and learned to hunt in areas where fire had caused fresh new growth to appear.

We know from our ancestors' teeth that they started out eating just about everything. No doubt fruits and buds were favored, just as with monkeys and all great apes today. The new niche fitted man's capacities so well that in both meat hunting and plant gathering our species excelled. Man proceeded to spread to most of the available land areas of the world. For an immensely long period of time (a million years or more) a remarkable degree of expertness and devotion characterized man the hunter. It is even possible that the numbers and capacities of men combined to bring about the extermination of several species of large mammals. That may have happened because such large mammals as mammoths, antelopes, and bison have relatively low reproductive rates. They also have other mammalian enemies, and their physical environments may have been deteriorating due to climatic changes.

An ecologist supposes that whatever the food base, the harvester sooner or later runs into trouble if he creates too many of his own kind. For man, the consequences of overharvesting must sometimes have led to starvation or to some kind of uncertainty that carried the threat of starvation. Even that best of all possible worlds, the food-rich savanna, had its limits. Our ancestors must have occasionally learned that limits operate for man, even with all his brains.

We must further suppose that there were many answers to the same question. No doubt one or another of the little family groups of men tried them all. Some hunters simply learned that if they bowed to the proper idols, babies were born abundantly.

They also apparently learned that if they killed off the babies that came when the going was rough, things went along fairly smoothly. It seems probable that, during most of the last million years, it ordinarily took 50,000 years for human populations to double, worldwide. (And there is considerable evidence that the deciding factor was human control, not disease, starvation, or predatory beasts.) We may, in passing, contrast that remarkable stability with today's doubling of world population every thirty-five years or so.

Other groups found out (by trying it and living to tell the tale) that they could support their larger numbers, even if the game mammals failed, by returning to a more herbivorous diet. In some cases, they emphasized fruits, in others, protein-rich grain seeds. Others gave up big game entirely and migrated to the seacoast, estuaries, and lakes and became relatively immobile consumers of fish and shellfish.

As a consequence of man's successes, the world became crowded, as well as less abundantly supplied with big game mammals. When the belly is empty and memory sharp, one group of people looks with disfavor upon groups of possible competitors. This causes groups to spread out. If, on the other hand, a group has a reliable field of wild grain or an oyster bed or salmon fishery, defense of it makes that group a stay-at-home. Defense, of course, works both ways. You impede the movements of others but you are not free to roam yourself. If you have chosen well, you cannot help establishing the beginnings of a city. If you have not chosen well, you will leave no one to mourn your poor judgment.

Chapter 4

Preparing to Feed Ourselves

The shift from being the world's most successful hunters to occupying Earth's first villages took a long time. Over the scores of thousands of years, the transition took place in many parts of the world. Resources were either husbanded or depleted.

Two sorts of plants were affected. Trees, especially those that produced fruit, like apple, citrus, cherry, date palm, olive, almond, were encouraged, and they thrived in stands of trees that ultimately became orchards. Weedy annual plants also benefited. Out of their number those chosen for cultivation showed some capacity for attracting man's favors, for avoiding his attentions, or of profiting from his brutal compacting of soil, breaking of sod, opening of forest canopy, or fearful burning orgies. Thus, weeds came to be thought of as the footprints of agricultural and village man.

Man may also have benefited some species of trees by driving plant-eating enemies away. On the other hand, the encouragement of certain plants may have acted as a snare that kept some species of animals within man's reach. Some of them at least occasionally became food. Some, such as the goat and cow, were ultimately domesticated.

With every success, there came population pressures that demanded a greater food base. The answer was always more territory or a more productive territory. The response of men to this imperative has never been simple. We have invented complicated guides to govern our slaughter of fellow mammals. Rules of sportsmanship are shadows of those ancient rituals. We have even invented rules to govern our slaughter of each other, although these frequently fail to apply to people whose land you must have. War, it may be noted, began a long time ago.

In spite of the ease with which people can be induced to enjoy a successful war—or the heightened competition of our cities—not all groups respond in that manner. Some relatively ancient groups, with admirable brains and beautiful tools, moved into higher-temperate latitudes. They were either avoiding competition or moving because of it. In those wintry and thus seasonally marginal habitats, they applied the hunting and gathering techniques that had always served man well. There, too, they found that an ounce of prevention was worth a pound of cure. They began to realize that a little cultivation and encouragement of the grains reaped benefits in larger harvests. The benefits were in the form of enough food for the harsh times when game was played out and no food could be had by trade or thievery from the old heartland of civilization. In the heartland, of course, there was little need to cultivate if you had access to land: such seed-rich grasses as wheat produced crops of surplus seed without cultivation. Necessity, not pure intelligence, was the mother of invention.

The plants, as living things always do, responded to the activities of man. They lost some of their primeval toughness becoming simultaneously tenderer as food and more vulnerable to pests—and dependent upon care by man. Wheat, for example, began to produce heads of grain that did not shatter as easily as they had when the plant was seeding itself, for their harvester now opened the ripened head at his own convenience and he favored only those plants (and their seeds) that complied with his needs and rhythms. Plants were similarly rewarded for ripening their grain all at once.

Over the course of thousands of years, agricultural knowledge accumulated among human tribes. Plants gained "wisdom" much more slowly—by genetic processes alone. Although this worked well for both parties, it should be observed that the several species involved, including man, were trading in food *webs* for food *chains*. The probable consequences of this action have already been alluded to.

With the domestication of the first forms of wheat, the age of grasses began. Whether two other staple grasses, rice and corn, were tamed by people who knew about cultivation of grains or if they were independent inventions is not clear. At any rate, man's swift 10,000-year development from the beginnings of recognizable cultivation to full-fledged urban culture and to today's urban crisis took place, by necessity, alongside the domestication of the special group of annual plants known as grasses.

Certain other species of plants were in a sense put onto the road to cultivation by wheat. At first, barley was just a weedy associate in wheat fields. When cultivators took their flocks and fields to more unfavorable, drier regions, wheat grew poorly, but barley flourished and thus became the primary crop. Rye and oats also took the easy road as man's associates, and they have ended up, like wheat, barley, and corn, unable to compete in nature. Modern corn long ago gave up even the natural ability to reseed itself and struck a dubious bargain with man for their mutual perpetuation.

The mutualism of men and grains led to a recognizable chain of events: good food, plentiful energy, more people. Villages and leaders emerged. Nuclear political units were established, and more complex governments and priestly hierarchies were not far behind. Tax collectors convinced cultivators of an ever-increasing need for more grain. These plants rewarded the added foresight and extra industry of men. The result was a highly developed social organization and a highly motivated technology that has reached without a break from the dim historical past into our own days.

As population pressures developed, constellations of villages spread over the surface of the habitable Earth. They spread with glacial slowness, adapting to first one environmental factor and then another. They left the sparsely forested primeval savannas. They carried with them both a distrust of, and a way of life not well fitted to, forest. They learned to create savannas of their own through forest clearing.

The assault upon vegetations created tame plants. It also brought forth the weeds that thrived upon disturbance. Some of these, like the poppy and various mustards, became new crops. Some, like dandelion, pigweed, and lamb's-quarter, have remained weeds, in spite of the fact that they make suitable food if properly prepared. The Middle East and Europe added figs, many sorts of beans, lentils, peas, flax, and gradually, many others. Men were making fairly intensive use of cereal grains by about 11,000 years ago in the Near East. All or nearly all significant domestication occurred in that long period of harsh schooling of civilization known as the Neolithic (or New Stone) Age. During this time, man moved out of his Ice Age caves and learned to make remarkably fine tools from stone. Somewhere around 11,000 to 10,000 years ago, he began to settle into modest villages. Men were still stocking their tables from normal hunting forays and from opportunistic plant gathering, but the way was being cleared for sustained plant cultivation.

Animal domestication was on the way, too. Dogs, for food or for partners in the chase, were domesticated some 11,000 years ago in the Near East. They were already social animals and readily adapted their behavior to human partners. Their arrival at entirely domestic status may have been preceded by the domestication of goats and sheep, however. Presumably sheep were tamed for food, for wild sheep were good for little else, since they had no wool to speak of. At about the same time, pigs became permanent partners of man in the enterprise of civilization. The oldest domesticated cattle known are from southeastern Europe (about 8,500 years ago). By about 5,200 years ago, cattle seem to have been pulling ploughs. Horses were latecomers, substantial evidence of their domestication appearing about 4,000 years ago.

These early events supplied man with the bread, meat, and

horsepower that energized his great leap into history as we know it. Only the last few minutes of technological time (and these mostly among affluent countries and classes) have changed the patterns of that employment of horsepower very much.

Chapter 5

The Birth of Cities

The first substantial sites of resident populations were intimately related not only to food sources but also to the vital nonfood natural resources, water and shelter. Chief among the ready-made sites were the elevated sedimentary plains, where rainfall was relatively light. There, soil was rich and grazing mammals such as bison, ancestral cattle, horses, and antelopes abounded. Such mammals have long interacted with fire to favor the dominance of grasslike vegetation. Also favorable were the areas near rivers that received regular baptismal floods and layers of rich sediment. There were, finally, the estuaries and deltas at the mouths of great rivers, then as now rich in fisheries that respond to the loads of nutrients brought down by rivers. Deltas at the mouths of lower-latitude and unglaciated rivers deserve particular attention, for they were nourished by watersheds where soil was little disturbed by glaciers.

Such points ultimately became the sites of cities: Paris,

London, Baghdad, Berlin, Peking, Moscow. All these were first village cultures, self-sufficient islands of local traditions and stubborn conservatism. How and why did they shift to the modern urban pace of kaleidoscopic change, to innovative leadership, and to consumption of materials?

Competition within a species spurs mobility. The development of new means of transportation accompanied the slow spread of man along rivers, coastlines, foothills, and grassland-forest edges. The first cities, natural product of mobility, change, jostling, and competition, were hub cities. They grew up from hub villages, located at points where trade routes met. Goods, people, energy, and information interacted. There was an inevitable fusion, blending, and synthesis of ideas. New materials and new products resulted. The city became an imposing (and defensible) repository of materials, which was a major reason for urban people to cling together and retain their new level of integration.

Yet the developing city was as much a window on the world as a repository of goods. It differed from the village of other times and other areas not so much in size as in having a world view as opposed to a parochial view. The first city to earn the name appears to have been Çatal Hüyük in south-central Asiatic Turkey. There, some 9,000 years ago, as James Mellaart has described it, a small village with a view became a highly developed community. Within about a thousand years, it evolved an elaborate religion, a sophisticated art, and a definite economic class structure. Following that thoroughly modern beginning, other villages, at strategic hubs and nubs and thoroughfares around the world, became cities. And all that we know of history followed.

Still, just why are cities where they are? Inspection of a map shows that villages and towns are not randomly situated; each has a reason for its site. It is not shallow determinism to say that every human aggregation is resource-oriented. In wetter areas, villages are located in drier places. In dry lands, they occupy damper sites. In cold countrysides, warmer exposures will tend to be chosen.

The siting of cities can be analyzed in other ways. Cities deal with ideas and materials on the move. Their success in accommodating that flow is molded by various environmental influences. Physiographic relief acts to "gate" the flow. Diagrams show what is meant. An unvaried environment, even when provided with "flow axes," is not likely to be the site of a city (Figures 1, 4). If land juts into water or water into land (Figures 2, 5), however, a city may well have its beginning. If two bodies of land, or two bodies of water, jut toward each other, a city may

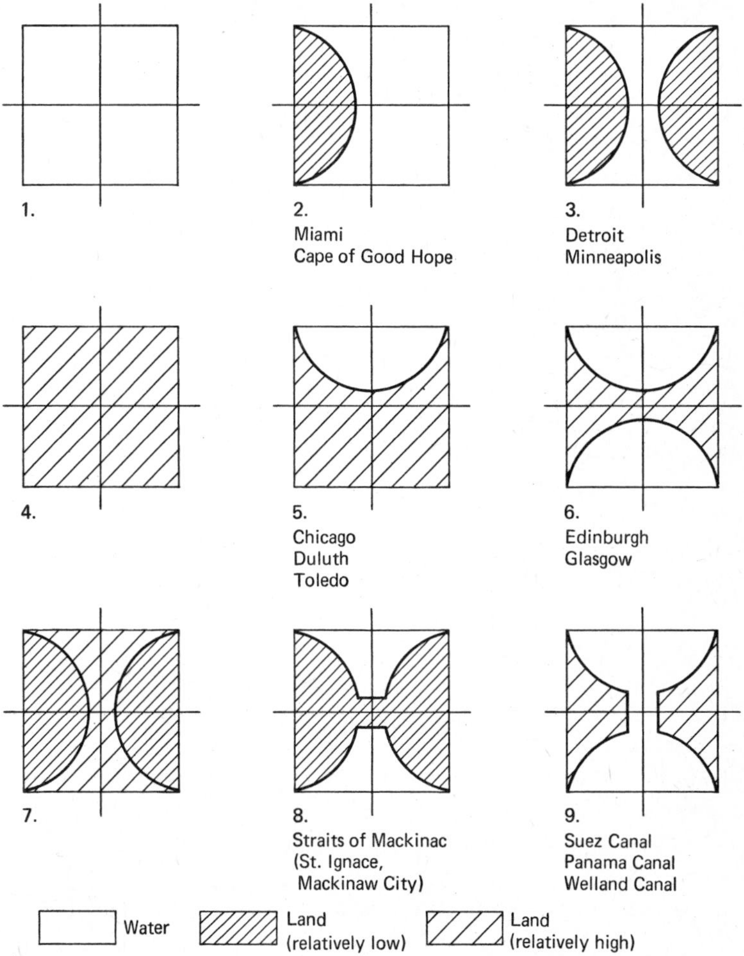

spring up (Figures 3, 6). Valleys that lie between constricting highlands (Figure 7) can clearly influence the sites of cities, and the effects of bridges and canals (Figures 8, 9) are easily imagined.

The "gates" that conduct the flow of ideas and materials may have zero, one, or two sides. They are usually zones of transition: water to land, flat land to mountainous country, marshland to drier areas, etc. Clearly, if you think about it, either the contiguous or the discontiguous axes may carry the preponderance of ideas or materials that are to be gated through a city. Furthermore, the degree of development and the direction of flow along each axis may differ in a distinctive manner from city to city. These dissimilarities are largely responsible for the variety that creates the vital personality of each city.

When the characteristics of a region induce the establishment of several residential centers, interaction between these centers follow. Curiously, the extent of this interaction closely parallels the general law of gravitational attraction between two bodies, that is, it depends upon the size of each "body" and the distance between. One can predict the number of telephone calls (H_e) between two cities, certainly one criterion of interaction, by the equation:

$$H_e = \frac{2.76\ P_1P_2}{d^{2\cdot 36}}$$

where P_1 and P_2 are the populations of the two cities and d is the distance between them. (The numbers are constants.) Cities which tend to communicate strongly with one another tend to grow together and, eventually, to fuse.

Lewis Mumford says that the size that a city can attain is somewhat governed by "the velocity and the effective range of communication." Since overcrowding actually interferes with effective communication, does this make the huge modern metropolis obsolete?

Chapter 6

Why the Circuit Is Overloaded

Stanley Milgram has pointed out that in Nassau County, a suburb of New York City: "One individual can meet 11,000 others within a 10-minute radius of his office by foot or car. In Newark, a moderate-sized city, he can meet 20,000 persons within this radius. But in midtown Manhattan he can meet fully 220,000."

It may be even better (or worse!) than that. If we consider the number of "interactive" individuals in a population, we have a certain number of possible interactive pairs, or dialogues. We may use the formula

$$D = \frac{N}{2}(N-1)$$

where D stands for the number of dialogues possible and N the number of individuals in the population. For a population of 10 persons, $D = 10/2(10 - 1)$, or 45. For a population of 100, $D = 4{,}950$. For a population of 1,000, $D = 499{,}500$. In other words, the number of possible dialogues increases a bit more than ten times as fast as the population.

According to Korzybski (and other early students of social and administrative sciences), matters are even more complicated. We may assume that the people with whom a given person has relations have, in their turn, relations with each other. Furthermore, each of these one-to-one interactions may have some functional interaction with other one-to-one interactions. The number of social events quickly becomes astronomical. Here the relevant formula is

$$R = N\left(\frac{2^N}{2} + N - 1\right)$$

where R is possible social events and N is number of individuals in the population. The relationship between number of people, assistants, or functions and the number of relationships or "problems" is given in the table below.

N	R
1	1
2	6
3	18
4	44
10	5,210

This readily accounts for the number of vice-presidents in banks, or the fact that bureaucrats work so inefficiently. It also explains why contagious diseases thrive upon human gatherings. Typhoid and tuberculosis bacteria, and such viral infections as measles and colds, do not persist except in cities.

The greater the number of people and the more wide-ranging their interactions, the greater are the opportunities for the working out of Korzybski's law. Of course there may be a negative correlation between the number of possible social events and smooth social functioning. Social breakdown may be facilitated by the very structure that now guarantees speedy transmission of people, ideas, and viruses. If so, we could expect the breakdowns to increase dramatically as population and population mobility increase.

There are other effects.

People have a limited amount of time. Dialogues, as they increase in number, become shorter in length and less profound in content. On the other hand, increased diversity of possible dialogues produces more and more interactions of high productivity; the formation of fertile subgroups is expedited. Thus, the city justifies itself, even today.

But for most urbanites a price must be paid. Interactions become highly formalized. Hospitality is reserved for the few persons you really know. Civility itself may become a rarity in public. Decisions may represent fiat more than organic processes of growth. This is not to say that no human needs are served. But it is possible that we have given "number of encounters" too high a priority.

It must also be said that "dialogue" implies exchange. Newspapers, TV, and radio are pretty much one-way flows, and hence are likely to wander from public consensus. They become propagandistic, operating at a low common denominator of "what the people want" and they provide little or no service to the leadership levels of society. The city dweller must contend not only with ever-increasing complexity but with a mercantile and political shaping of public taste by orators and advertisers. Both conditions short-circuit creative processes.

Cities are centers of the mass media that shape attitudes that have come to be called urban. In turn, these attitudes dictate what can be "news," and affect populations, urban and rural alike. The message is reinforced and amplified by what it molds. In ecological terms, this means positive feedback and exponential growth and it spells trouble. We are now suffering the effects of this kind of runaway process in the electric power–electric apparatus–consumer triangle. The media say buy, consumers buy. The public demands power and power companies legitimize the demand by urging increased consumption. Media men, manufacturers, and power companies grow in strength, their messages crowding out more vital information. Eventually, every home is filled with power-consuming goods; newspaper, TV, and radio messages are resplendent with urgent nonsense; power companies are taxed to their utmost to produce more and more electrical energy. And then the system ruptures wide open. In the presence of a strong federal subsidy such as defense subsidy, the process occurs more rapidly and when such subsidies are taken away, collapse occurs all the faster. When breakdown comes as in the case of the Lockheed industry of Seattle men lose jobs, and factories shut down, and the effects are felt in every sector of the economy. The buy and sell message, untempered by real dialogue, produces wild fluctuations.

Urbanization continues. As we have seen, although the modern city is one result of the growth of efficiency in communication, the problems of the city have grown as the complexity of communication has increased. Is there some way of increasing efficiency of constructive communication in such a way that problems can be sorted out and perhaps solved? Can we learn to keep communication unfettered? Can we, for example, separate information and manufacturing, so that we can have more of the former and only what we need of the latter? Can we consider ways of bringing closer together those who produce and those who consume?

Men desire rich and varied sensory experiences in nature. They search for orientation at the deeply personal level. Are great material wealth and hectic participation in information transfer (of the sort that the city provides) necessary for these? Would men not be better served by less consumption, or at least consumption of materials that are lovingly crafted and which last a long time? Must we continue to allow the means of communication to be exploited for the benefit of a relatively few corporations that continually say *consume, consume, consume,* when this, in turn, commits the society and its labor forces to ever greater production of whatever the corporations tell them to produce. Must we wait for the obstructionism and violence of a frustrated majority of urban souls to force us to change? These people are unable to participate effectively in the information game and they are, in some ways cheated by it. They manufacture and buy and sell: but they profit little. Not only is their share small of the bounty that an abundance of information seems to make possible; they are maimed by being cut off both from meaningful communication with each other and from nature.

Self-aggrandizement and self-profiting are ancient and even highly respected evils that we may have to forego. The presumptuous but showy selfishness of a few still charms the masses—but not into silence! Their interest is now, understandably, to be affluent, whether they have the means or capacity to command the necessary information of the urbanized world or not. The status of pollution alone in the modern world should be enough to warn us that extreme affluence for everyone, when numbers are so large, is impossible. A shift to new life styles that feature nonpolluting and nonexploitative richness is overdue. In any case, critical evaluation of how many people we can accommodate is vital for our success.

Part Three

The Potter and the Pot

Unless one merely thinks man was intended to be an all-conquering and sterlizing power in the world, there must be some general basis for understanding what it is best to do. This means looking for some wise principle of co-existence between man and nature, even if it has to be a modified kind of man and a modified kind of nature.

Charles S. Elton
The Ecology of Invasions by Animals and Plants

Man is prone to believe that there must exist some form of energy with a self-perpetuating power.

Nicholas Georgescu-Roegen
The Entropy Law and the Economic Process

Chapter 7

Who the Potter, Who the Pot?

"We shape our buildings and afterwards our buildings shape us," said Winston Churchill. As for cities, there is no doubt that the second part of the proposition applies, but there is little really substantial evidence that the first part still holds. This part of the urban dialogue is very one-sided.

The city, notable for its buildings, gobbles up open space, air, and sunlight. Park land is often seized for gas, highway, water, sewer, and other rights-of-way. Almost every urban park in the country is threatened today, and if not today, it will be tomorrow. Once all the space for lateral expansion is gone, building proceeds into the sky, blotting out air and sunlight for the structures below.

The buildings take on the aspect of huge trees fighting for their places in the forest canopy, the only difference being that, in the forest, every tree is designed into the system as a whole and rarely assumes a towering and arrogant posture. Each forest tree is not only designed to grow. It is designed to be taken apart.

Show us a major office building which has been planned for efficient destruction! The result, of course, is a rigidification of the total urban structure that strongly limits city planning in both space and time. It begins to look as if the buildings themselves, not the city planners, are pretty much in control of what happens next. The influence of the abiotic features of the city, of course, reach well beyond the buildings themselves—some say all the way to a differentiated city dwelling "type."

The American environment (not entirely an urban matter, of course) has sometimes been given the credit for certain changes in people migrating from other lands. However, it is not really clear why American-born children of immigrants, especially Jewish and Japanese groups, not only grew to an average height of 2 inches more than their parents but even experienced changes in head form (longer and shorter on the average than the parental types). There is, for example, some evidence that general stature of Europeans has increased since the days of armored knights. American college students are taller and heavier than those of twenty to thirty years ago. Better diets and other influences may, of course, be at work both in America and in Europe. On the other hand, it is quite possible that hybrid vigor and the working out of genetic trends are basically involved. In Norway, for example, girls mature earlier than they did only a century ago. Somewhat the same thing seems true of English and American girls. That it is purely a matter of improved diet is rather questionable since their earlier maturation now only equals that of most non-European populations, many of whom are far from well nourished.

We know little about the genetic effects of putting small numbers of people in new environments. That they represent only a small sample of genes (and are, therefore, likely to be unrepresentative of their home group), is clear. They also acquire a few new genes through intermarriages with other peoples. There is new food, possibly from better soil. There may be less, or at least different, work. It must also be considered that people of a certain genetic makeup possibly move more readily in the first place.

We should like to know if people in cities are fatter than their country cousins, other things being equal—and fatter at what ages? Are they taller or shorter, weaker or stronger? Do sex ratios change? What about the ages at which significant events occur: ages of women at sexual maturity, marriage, first child delivery, entry into the labor market, departure from the labor market, menopause, death? What about men?

Are there significant differences in life schedules? And how do these affect individual persons? For example, the urban environment tends to obscure seasonal differences. It floods life with artificial light and throws twenty-four-hour rhythms out of kilter.

How does natural (or shall we call it unnatural) selection occur today in man? There seems to have been a Darwinian selection of an urban "type" as urbanization became a more and more pervasive part of our lives. Survival of such a "fitter" group does not require that the less fit die off dramatically. It requires even less that we should consider the survivors in any way more admirable people than their predecessors. It merely means that they reproduce even a fraction of a percentage point better than other segments of the total population.

People entered the New Stone Age divided into numerous biologically distinct populations. It is unlikely that differences would have existed without good genetic, cultural, and environmental reasons, and people lived in social groups designed to maintain their differences.

Furthermore, the first substantial coming together of interacting cultures was probably not a grand homogenization. Villages blended into one political unit, but villagers from different places, as genetic units, may have mixed no more freely with one another than water mixes with oil. Instead, social groups slid over one another. They kept the genes in their own particular "pools." They probably had to, in the main, since their genes determined to some extent what they were best able to do and it was no doubt necessary to do the best they could.

Look at the environment of urban man. The pedestrian surfaces are hard. Feet suffer. Do really rural people have as much foot trouble as urban persons? If so, are the troubles the same? Consider the possibility that standing long periods of time may induce varicose veins and other malfunctions in the lower limbs. Is the capability to stand all day at a cash register distributed precisely equally among all body builds and all social groups? One could ask similar questions about stresses of the hip, eye, skin, ears, lungs, and every other part of the human body. We know relatively little, for example, about the presence of kidney stones as a variable dependent on the quality of water supply, food supply, and life style.

What other facets of ourselves might be molded by environmental variables? One of the most discouraging facts about the carelessness of our reworking of Earth is that we routinely learn so little from the massive experiments to which we carelessly expose ourselves and others. Even in our age of science, men who attempt to assess the effects of urban technologies upon "primitive" peoples are likely to be considered unprogressive and antiscientific.

Chapter 8

The Shaping of the Pot

Urbanization invevitably changes landscapes, even when people have the best of intentions. Forest and grasslands are the sources of our success, but their wild qualities always deteriorate under man's exploitative attentions. Urban changes, unlike those brought about by farmers and herdsmen, are noted for the totality of their impact. Nature is left, at least temporarily and locally, incapable of a remedial response.

Even primitive men changed their environments, sometimes drastically. As a carnivore, man competed with wolves and lions. He destroyed or was joined by such lesser carnivorous lights as dogs and cats. Herbivorous mammals felt man's influences, first as food source and then as objects of domestication, and some species may even have become extinct. Carnivores that ate man's domesticated animals, and herbivorous competitors with goats, sheep, and cattle, were all early labeled as enemies.

With agriculture, permanent vegetations were broken up and

soils often began to deteriorate. In addition to agricultural plants, annual weeds were favored. The ancient camp-following weeds from Europe (dandelion, dock, and pigweed) have tagged along after Western man everywhere he has gone. Some native opportunists also qualify as weeds. Asters and goldenrods are examples, although the most successful native American in this category is probably ragweed.

The establishment of modern urban areas and roads accelerates both physical and biotic breakdown. Topsoil is removed, eroded, or capped with concrete and houses. A 45-acre parking lot near Schenectady, New York, effectively stopped the soaking of some 40 inches of annual precipitation into the ground, and made its percolation into underground waterways minimal. The resulting runoff represents a total local loss of some 51 million gallons a year. As elsewhere, the short-sighted solution is to get water into storm sewers as soon as possible. Storm sewers become the circulatory systems of the new urban ecosystem. They may even expand and spread out to take in small streams that are then entirely encased in underground pipes. Specifically, the storm sewers leading away from such ground-covering constructions as large parking lots carry not only potentially useful water but also a witches' brew of gasoline, oil, and grime from cars, a flush of human filth, and salt and sand from winter deiceing operations.

Accelerated, immediate runoff of water increases movement of sediments. Soil is thus lost. The resulting silt, if it accompanies water into a lake or pond, shades out submerged vegetation. Suspended silt in water reduces stability of streams. It insures a shorter life for dams and the impoundments of water above them, for the latter quickly fill up with silt.

The vegetation of population centers declines. It is replaced by buildings and roads. Many species of native plants cannot tolerate trampling and soil compaction. Sensitive species are killed by changes in atmospheric conditions, especially the increase of ozone, fluorides, and sulfurous gases. Evergreen conifers (pines, spruces, and firs) are easily harmed by air pollutants, as are many cultivated flowering and agricultural plants. Our own safety might encourage us to cut back on air pollution when pines die, rather than to let people sell us the notion of planting more resistant species of trees. We might also consider the wisdom of insisting on keeping our air clean enough to grow such pollution-sensitive vegetables as spinach, parsley, celery, and chard uninjured.

With the loss of vegetation, surfaces dry out faster and there is reduced thermal buffering. This means that built-up areas heat and cool more rapidly than under wilderness conditions.

Buildings are biotic centers of a sort. They act as caves and serve to house more than men. Rats, mice, lice, bedbugs, fleas, crickets, silverfish, and cockroaches are examples. Mice are rarely pleasant companions. Rats can carry plague and are hosts to fleas. Lice and bedbugs may be disease vectors. Cockroaches may not carry diseases, but they are less than desirable to most people.

Pigeons and starlings find cities acceptable supplements to their natural dwelling sites. Peregrine falcons might do likewise but for the disturbances they receive from people who do not like hawks. Nighthawks have long utilized flat roofs of city buildings, substituting them for the barren fields that are their natural habitat. Most cities, however, are not favorable for them, probably because of the abundance of pesticides that kill their prey and interfere with their reproduction.

Buildings also have ledges, seemingly tailormade for lichens and such climbing plants as various ivies. But here, again, the deterioration of modern cities is evident, for even the notoriously hardy lichens die, probably as a consequence of air pollution.

After the primal landscape has been stripped, the city spreads and rises. Spreading is more of the same; rising creates a new set of problems. Huge structures such as the twin 1,350-foot towers of the World Trade Center on the southwest shore of Manhattan lead the surge into the skies. With completion of the 1,450-foot-high Sears Roebuck building in Chicago, the Center's towers will, however, be second best.

People follow their offices skyward, and apartment living is not far behind. The 100-story Hancock Center is 1,127 feet high and is equipped to house its 1,700 tenants such that they will never have to leave—their "every requirement" can be satisfied within the building.

Such structures stand in the way of migrating birds and sway more than a foot in strong winds. Residents and workers find themselves above the clouds at times, living in isolation from familiar landmarks of concrete, vehicles, street sounds, and soil.

Buildings like these consume vast amounts of material in their construction, and their enormous consumption continues every day of their existence. The World Trade Center consumes more electricity than the city of Schenectady, the "home town" of the mighty General Electric Company with its many manufacturing and research and development facilities. The Center will eventually house concentrations of 130,000 workers and visitors each day. That crowd will generate 50 tons of garbage and 2.25 million gallons of sewage daily—about the same as the entire city of Stamford, Connecticut.

For reasons that seem more related to prestige and showmanship than to human behavior, big companies continue to make big buildings. Big buildings challenge the human psyche in new ways. Some people find life in the clouds anxiety-ridden, and dislike the shaking, swaying, and vibrations. Others fear an increased incidence of muggings, burglaries, and rape, crimes that are made easier by the hallways, elevators, and other isolated chambers.

Views are obstructed, of course, but new to the skyscraper problem is a phenomenon known as TV shading. The new Sears tower recently transferred the TV antennae from the Hancock buildings to its summit, at the cost of $5 million, because TV reception for some 60,000 households had deteriorated.

These towers of concrete, glass, and stone also channel winds and create dangerous gusts at street level. Designers of some larger structures have installed railings along sidewalks to protect pedestrians.

The skyscraper symbolizes much of our problem: centralization, estrangement, blind growth. With all this, however, owners of the Empire State Building may add another eleven floors to their structure, in order to make it again the world's tallest building!

Chapter 9

Stoking the Urban Furnace

Energy is an old story. Without the constant output of energy from the sun, there would be no life on Earth. Energy is always on the move. After its temporary capture in organic molecules, or its brief use in warming Earth, energy is soon on its way back into the heat trap of the open universe.

But it is a common error to believe that efficiency of energy use is increasing in the United States. On the contrary, it now costs more energy to produce a potato, more to ship the potato, more to buy the potato, more to process the potato, more to store it on grocers' shelves. Trip distances are increasing, for all materials at all levels. Increasing amounts of energy are used in manufacturing metals to make the machines that have themselves increased in numbers. Everywhere there are more tractors, computers, harvesters, processors, packagers. We allow ourselves to be sold aluminum throwaway cans, even though it is much more expensive, in terms of energy required, to manufacture an aluminum can than to recycle one.

The city man thinks of energy in terms of electricity, oil, gas, and coal. These energy types so dwarf the small amounts of heat energy needed to stoke the working man's bodily furnace that it is understandable that we ignore that type of energy. It is estimated that one hard-working adult man expends some 3,000 kilocalories of energy per day. This amounts to a little over a pound of refined food, more or less dispersed in 5 pounds of water, daily.

It costs no more to feed a working man that it ever did, in terms of calories. The economic energy budget of urban America, however, does not depend on consumption of man-calories. The most urgent factor to consider is depletion of capital, in the form of permanent loss of nonrenewable fossil fuels.

Our society presents a vast array of automobiles, washing machines, electric dryers, toasters, elevators, trains, air conditioners, enormous construction devices, looms, mills, and the like. Each is an energy user and each requires a great deal of energy to put it onto the street or into the home or factory. These machines make the urban world run. It is through them that we push most of the energy that we capture. In terms of electricity alone, Americans used 1.06 trillion kilowatts in 1965. (A kilowatt, or kilowatt hour, is the standard unit used in measuring electricity; a 100-watt bulb uses a kilowatt hour of electricity in ten hours.) About 1.52 trillion kilowatt hours were used in 1970. For 1990 the projected figure is 5.83 trillion kilowatt hours. The recent trend is for the per capita consumption of electricity to double every ten years. Keep in mind that the number of people also increases yearly—and that the figures given are only for America, not for the other 95 percent of a populous, often energy-starved world.

Yet, what are we doing about the implications of this? We are tearing across the North Slope of Alaska, eager to open up petroleum reserves that we shall need much more, even as fuel, at a later time than we do now. Recall that nature has spent hundreds of millions of years evolving and storing the complex hydrocarbon molecules of petroleum. The results of our use of these molecules is to degrade them—and, at the moment, mostly for very low purposes. Those complex molecules are vitally important in lubrication and the manufacture of plastics. The future may also see petroleum as a food source using special bacteria. What a waste to continue to turn most of them into simple carbon dioxide or carbon monoxide! Not only is the waste of fuel disastrous, the pollution that results is enormous. While exhaustion of gasoline may do for the internal combustion engine what concern for our health has not been able to do, the result may be catastrophic. It will force us (and there will be many more of us then) to turn to inadequately tested and perhaps dangerous forms of energy production.

Some 2 billion of the Earth's people do not have electricity at their fingertips. They thus lack the "mechanical slaves" that we take for granted. The number of such slaves can be calculated, very roughly, if we compute the energy expended by a hard-working man (3,000 kcal) per day, multiply this by 365, divide this into the total amount of energy consumed as electricity, and then divide the resulting figure by the approximately 200 million people in our country. The figure comes out to be something like forty-five electricity slaves. This is only part of the story, however, for we consume some eight times as much energy in the form of gas, ten times as much energy in the form of crude petroleum, and five times as much in soft coal. As of 1968, the grand total was something like 980 slaves. By these calculations, we have arrived, quite properly we think, at a figure that is nearly twice as high as the 500 or so energy slaves commonly attributed to each of us. How do you feel about the fact, reported by Buckminster Fuller, that the average Asian person commands only three energy slaves? (In Asia, 56 percent of the world's population (1960) used only about 10 or 12 percent of the energy expended by the world.) Or the fact that by 1969, the United States representing 5.7 percent of the world's population, was consuming 29.9 percent of the world's crude oil?

That all this slavery transpires without degradation of the environment is not likely. The saga of the automobile and the internal-combustion engine will be touched upon later. Fossil fuel used in generating electricity now contributes 50 percent of the dangerous sulfur oxides and about 25 percent of the particulates polluting the air. The cooling of generating equipment uses about 80 percent of all cooling water consumed by industry. The heat so dissipated becomes thermal pollution. By 1980, the power industry will require the equivalent of about one-sixth of the total available freshwater runoff in the nation for use as cooling fluid. If this is dumped into the nonurban environment, water quality for many purposes will be impaired.

The sun is our prime source of energy. Some of that solar energy is fixed in photosynthetic reactions. All organisms, including plants, then use that fixed energy to run all their living processes. Only plants, however, are producers. There is also a relatively small amount of fossil solar energy in the form of petroleum, coal, and lignite. This has accumulated over the last 300 million years or so. The breaking up of this rich store has supported the worldwide spread of Western civilization.

If we wish Western civilization to continue, we must find a way to solve some problems related to energy use. Fossil fuels, upon which we depend so heavily now, are strictly limited. For the Age of Energy to continue, we must learn to tap sources of energy, such as nuclear power produced in various kinds of reactors, some of which are as yet only theorized. M. King Hubbert of the United States Geological Survey estimates that world petroleum products may be substantially exhuasted within 100 years from now. Coal will probably last as a practical source of energy only a few hundred years at most; not only is much of it of poor quality, but it must also be remembered that coal will not last long if we have to shift largely to it as an energy source. This makes it appear that fossil fuel as an energy source will soon be unavailable. In the absence of radical breakthroughs in nuclear power development regarding bioaccumulation of radioactive materials, disposal of waste heat, and the resource base, energy sources will then be inadequately researched solar engines, tidal and waterfall power, heat from the Earth (geothermal power), and, of course, photosynthesis, which got us started in the first place. But none of these (or any combination of them) will support many of the kind of spendthrift energy wasters that Americans now are.

We are more interested at the moment in illustrating vividly the enormous role that energy plays in our lives, especially in cities, than in trying to digest the claims and counterclaims put forth by various prophets.

Obviously, not all energy sources are of equal rank, safety, or usefulness. In spite of the small amount of it that we as biological units require, it is photosynthesis alone that makes it possible for us to live and to regulate and control the flow of other forms of energy. Cities, as prime centers for energy control for the entire surface of Earth, are thus either directly or indirectly dependent upon green plants. That we are at present living far beyond the energy budget is another matter.

Just how in the world do we use so much energy? Let's take a critical look at the expenditure of energy in building an apartment, say your own. Make a list of every kind of material found in your residence and the weight of each: wood, stone, copper, steel, lead, glass, fabric, cement, slate, asphalt, rubber, asbestos, fiberglass, etc. Then approximate the height of the center of gravity for each substance as it now stands. You can then compute the energy expenditure for the local placing of the assorted materials in terms of work: force times distance. The figures increase remarkably for those living well above the ground. A two-story building costs *more* than twice the energy to build as a one-story one, just in terms of energy required to raise materials into place. There are also additional costs, such as elevators.

Next, consider sources of each material in terms of whether its handling is primary, secondary, tertiary, and so on. That is, how many steps is it from its original condition? Approximate (you will need a research library, a desk calculator, and a lot of time) the amount of refining that has gone on. How many tons of ore yield a ton of copper for electric wiring? Add to this the energy consumption per unit of distance moved in transport. The latter will get you into the practical world of 20-ton trucks that travel 5 miles per gallon of diesel fuel. From there you must figure the kilocalories of energy released by use of the motor fuel and convert this figure into units of work accomplished.

Consider the number of man-hours needed to process the steel used in building your home—the quarrying of the ore, its processing in smelters, the special treatment given the steel before it is finally cut or pressed into a product that can be used in building. Remember that at each step along the way energy is used to keep buildings heated, furnaces running, engines at work, machines operating. In addition, you may then calculate the caloric value of such organic materials as boards or slabs of plastic, that is, the amount of solar energy that went into their fabrication in the primary synthesis.

If you really make a thorough analysis, you will find that your apartment has ties with most parts of the region, state, nation, and world. The parts have been complexly routed to you. Consider the wanderings of Danish teak furniture, in view of the fact that no teak grows in Denmark; or think of the Japanese stereo unit made of Great Lake steel and Appalachian coal.

Weigh the luxury of such a house compared to a log cabin that you and your neighbors would have erected a couple of centuries ago. What do you think that the house would have cost if you had really paid (that is, "internalized") all the costs of industrial pollution along the way? Could you have afforded to pay all the workers, here and abroad, really affluent wages? Could you have built it at all if appropriate provisions had been made to prevent exploitation of nonrenewable resources for private profit?

The house is built. What then? There is the maintenance of acres of glass in modern buildings, walls to be painted regularly, roofs to be kept in repair. Do architects tell you how much window washers are going to cost—not this year alone but every year for generations?

Every new house becomes an old one. Windows get dirty; paint peels. Timbers are dented, infested with termites, and riddled by mildews. Glass breaks, beams sag. Smells invade, pollutants creep in. Even the best keeper eventually finds himself with a liability on his hands.

Thus, a building that was a measurable burden to the world at large in its infancy remains a burden for its lifetime. It is a burden in death and a burden in resurrection, for, when the time comes to replace it, it must first be displaced.

Think of the cost of displacing the Old Metropolitan Opera House or the Empire State Building. That, remember, is energy that we might like to spend on other things. Perhaps engineers, who have made great strides in decreasing costs of manufacturing things, will begin to look for efficient ways to reassemble and reuse things and parts of things. So far, prefabrication of whole units or parts of units is very exciting. But the leftovers from the displacement of modern buildings are often less readily disposable or reusable than bricks, building stones, or timbers. There seems no reason why we could not build structures of unit-bits that could be used over and over. What an ecological boon it would be if we could use the constituent materials of old structures, already on site, in the building of the new.

POSTSCRIPT: REFLECTIONS ON THE ETHICS OF ENERGY

Energy is the ultimate coin. All materials that we use are the agents of energy. All man-made things are transformations of these primary resources. The surface array of man-made things (the whole urban-rural human scene that resources make possible) deserves our respect much less than the foundation upon which they are built.

There is, as any leftist will tell you, a threat from the idle rich, for they command and misuse vast armies of energy slaves. But there is a far vaster number of energy slaves that will be commanded by the much more numerous middle- and upper-lower-class persons. The latter make up a very substantial part of our households and numbers. They also represent the part of the population that, barring social breakdown, is far more likely than either the very rich or the very poor to grow richer (and hence use more energy) in the years immediately ahead. They make up the bulk of the workers at the great Albany Mall project. They are the buyers of air conditioners, trail bikes, power lawnmowers, snowmobiles, second cars, suburban ranch houses, and extraurban second homes that are vacant most of the year. This does not mean that other, poorer people will not want air conditioners. If they get them, justice may be served; but they then join the pollutors.

A little thought will reveal the connections between the growth of consumption and the use of energy. The depth of our concern, as ecologists, is greater even than our desire for peace. It is greater than our personal desire for an end to the spector of rationing of parks, airplane fares, cars, and houses. The ecological basis for the kind of world we should like to have is being undermined. The villain is our attitudes that appear not to know how to maintain conditions necessary for our system's perpetuation. What will happen as more people are born? First of all, there will be more unproductive young people in the population, requiring more schools and other energy-using services but paying no taxes. (For example, 48 percent of Costa Rica's rapidly growing population is under fifteen years of age; in some rapidly growing countries, there will shortly be fifty people for each ten new jobs.) If we internalize costs, the costs of goods and services will increase unless we stop using some of the goods and services. What will happen to our already feeble efforts to increase incomes for really poor people? What will it profit the latter when they find that the larger incomes of those above them have inflated the economy to the point where increased salary is no longer an increase in real income.

Most of us still talk as if the physical, technological solutions known to us or dreamed of by us are possible. We had better act under the assumption that this is not true. Under the flag of Progress, we have been marching in locked step. We have been told to say that it is good. But consider that Progress includes Lake Erie. Have the bison, parakeet, and dodo actually been "sacrificed to progress," as we are often told? Or have we just been cutting up and feeding our life-supporting system to a force that we no longer control?

Ultimately, our thinking must include not just cities but the entire planet. Energy use in industrial (or other) activity must be limited not only because of pollution and resource depletion but also, eventually, because of the amount of heat released. We are already worrying about how to get rid of heat produced by power generation. Even when heat is disposed of, it is usually in an undesirable manner. Rivers, often tagged for prime recreation areas by planners for the future, may thus by the year 2000 be uninhabitable for many of the species of life that we shall wish to keep. Some people have supposed that when the amount of man-made heat released into the atmosphere reaches something like 1 percent of the amount of incident solar energy flux at the Earth's surface, unpredictable (and certainly uncontrollable) fluctuations in weather will be generated on a continentwide scale. There is a possibility that the energy released by man may already be 1/2,500 of the radiation balance at the surface of the Earth. Remember that this is happening at a time when very few people in the world have anything like the number of energy slaves they want and when the number of people in the world may double in less than thirty-five years.

In spite of the great amount of popular propaganda about the desirability of changing climates, the likelihood is that the biggest changes will be unintended ones. Like all side effects, these are not really "side" effects at all, but effects of enormous importance that we would simply rather not hear about. The effects of energy wastage already have us worried. It looks as if most of the know-how of weather control will shortly be absorbed to eliminate the man-made bad weather.

We have, it appears, confused power needs with power addiction. Power addiction has fostered an economy based not only upon waste of materials (so much that we now manufacture is unnecessary), but waste of time and energy in supplying those materials, not to mention the energy expended in containing and channeling waste materials and waste energy. At a great many levels of our economy, prevention of waste will make us fear for our jobs: thus our very natural fear of unemployment binds us further to waste. And increased technological efficiency in resource retrieval and processing simply masks the increasing overhead costs of leaner ores hauled over greater distances.

What will the results be? And are there ways out?

Chapter 10

The Air of the City

Building any structure does something to the nearby climate. Indeed, that is the primary reason we build. But there may be unintended effects of great significance, many of them unpleasant. Structures increase shadowing, decrease ventilation, contain and intercept sound, and decrease evaporative cooling. They also often exert a "greenhouse effect" and produce unbearably high temperatures, especially if much glass is used. These inadvertent changes are added to the effects of unwise (or, at least, uncomfortable) siting of cities. The total result can be a rather unpleasant, man-made microclimate, which, although "micro" on a global scale, is still the place where we live most of our lives. We fight off its effects by using air conditioners, heaters, air static reducers, dust removers, humidifiers, perfumers, dehumidifiers, and the like. All such devices require energy to build and install. Most of them require a constant input of energy to keep them going year after year. Peak summer use of air conditioning in New York City is now so great that upstaters have to cut down on their own use of electricity to make it possible. In addition, certain kinds of air conditioners use the cooling power of water that runs, one-way, through them. A 3-ton unit of this type may use 2,900 gallons of water per eight-hour day.

Riverine city sites such as New York and St. Louis probably never had really delightful summer climates. There is, however, plenty of evidence that cities themselves have made matters worse. The evidence is summarized briefly below from work by climatologist H. E. Landsberg and systems ecologist K. E. F. Watt.

Several changes in the man-level climate of cities follow the building of the city. Surfaces are reduced in area (a plain building instead of a leafy tree). Surfaces harden (concrete and steel are everywhere and water is quickly shed). There is replacement of organic materials that heat slowly by concrete and metal that heat and cool quickly. Heat, produced inside the city by men and machines, is retained by the city, especially in its asphalt and in its ill-ventilated chambers. Furthermore, there is a pooling of increased amounts of noxious gases, active chemicals, and solids in the air. No wonder that one man described the city as something like a volcano. The result is in almost all ways a deterioration of the outdoor urban climate.

Solar radiation suffers a 15 to 20 percent reduction in cities, with one-third or more of this occurring within the building levels. The rest is reflected or absorbed by dusts and gases. There may be an almost total elimination of ultraviolet irradiation. What does this do to the vitamin D normally produced by ultraviolet irradiation of our food and our bodies? Apparently, we must now depend entirely upon pills and "enriched" bread for this important vitamin. Illumination (that is, the visual effects of solar radiation) may be reduced in cities by up to 50 percent of its normal amount. Visual range is reduced as a result of fogs and haze. In the world's big cities, there was a doubling of the number of days with fog during the fifty years previous to 1930. That this need not have been quite so bad is now clear. Stricter control over the kinds of fuels used in heating and industry has alleviated the condition in many modern cities: Pittsburgh, St. Louis, and

London are examples. However, conditions may worsen if we return to lower-quality fuels.

Little is now known about the effects of differences in atmospheric electric properties. There are changes. The percentage of small ions (charged submolecular particles) in city air is 50 to 75 percent less than in the country. The number of large, charged particles (small ions quickly attach to suspended particulates) is on the order of ten times as great. This increases the electrical potential gradient, since more positively than negatively charged ions accumulate in our microclimate. The consequences, if any, of this two- or threefold increase in electrical potential are still unclear. At any rate, positive ionization is one product of combustive processes. This tends to replace the normally negatively charged air. It is believed by some that such air inhibits the body's capacity to expel pollutant particles by immobilizing cilia of bronchial tubes. Some evidence also indicates that certain kinds of psychological depression accompany exposure to positive ionization.

The situation with regard to precipitation is very complicated, but there appears to be a definite increase of perhaps up to 10 percent in total precipitation over heavily urbanized regions. There is also an increase of perhaps 10 percent in the number of days with small amounts of precipitation. However, if pollution by small particulates becomes great enough, a new pattern may emerge. The number of cloudy days may increase, but there may be too many condensation nuclei for rain to fall at all because the droplets formed are so small.

Patterns of snowfall may change dramatically in two ways. First, the somewhat higher temperatures of cities may cause precipitation to fall as rain rather than snow. There may be as many as 25 percent more days with snow outside than inside the city. But the presence of increasing numbers of condensation nuclei may result in an increase of snow in a particular snowstorm. Serious urban breakdowns are thus encouraged by the urban environment itself.

Temperature changes have been inadequately recorded in the kind of detail needed to establish the reality of changes. This tends, as a matter of fact, to be true of other environmental measurements. The result is a serious lack of solid baselines to judge our position. Changes in radiative processes, in absorption, in evaporation, convection, and turbulence all contribute to the final picture. The "city effect" alone is often hard to isolate and measure. Internal heating is, as yet, probably a negligible factor except locally. What is enormously effective in increasing heat in the city, however, is the great reduction in evaporative surfaces when vegetation, particularly forest, is removed and replaced with buildings and concrete with less surface area and with surfaces that will not soak up and release moisture. The trees also have great pollution-collecting leaf surface and they can add materially to our comfort and health. (They also add to our problems when leaves are raked and deposited by the city disposal services in ways that overload local areas with the toxic chemicals that the rotted leaves release; but that is another story.)

Removal of vegetation is also closely related to the fact that there is a reduction of around 6 percent in relative humidity in the city. This is due partly to higher temperatures and partly to rapid runoff of water, impervious surfaces, and the absence of moisture-replenishing plants.

Cloudiness increases over cities, due both to fog and to turbulence (that is, to rising of heated air until it cools and condenses). This is especially true in winter. In the first half of this century, large cities in the northern hemisphere experienced a 40 percent decrease in the number of clear days.

Winds, definitely a factor in the creature comfort of people, are also changed by cities. Speeds of winds are reduced by 25% or more, except in certain channels where buildings magnify and funnel annoying, dusty drafts. The frequency of calms increases by perhaps 20 percent, and summers are thereby made less bearable. In winter, when winds are needed to disperse pollutants, air quality may be particularly bad. However, winds are modified by effects of turbulence, and high buildings may produce enough turbulence so that a city can shift considerable amounts of heat into the outer air. It is even claimed that a one-story city with a 50 percent plant area might be cooler in the daytime than bare, flat, unvegetated countryside.

That you do not have to wait long for your city to produce its own climate is shown by studies of H. E. Landsberg. In just two years, in the widely publicized "new town" of Columbia, Maryland, surface temperatures were already ten degrees above surrounding fields, and forests and sulfur dioxide levels had increased 10 percent. No doubt conditions are worse in local, restricted areas.

One of the hopes of decently housing future populations and helping populations now living hinges on the building of new towns. The questions become: Can you keep people and industry from irresponsibly polluting the new towns? Can you keep people from capitalizing on a good thing and selling their spacious vegetated lots for suburban developments and high-rise apartments?

Much has been written about the particles urban man puts into his atmosphere. In 1971 the highly urbanized state of Pennsylvania released into its air 5,045,500 tons of sulfur oxides; 5,877,300 tons of carbon monoxide; 1,164,600 tons of hydrocarbons; 1,460,200 tons of nitrous oxide; and 2,321,900 tons of particulates. A white shirt does not remain white long where such concentrations of particulates exist. But there are other effects from such mushrooming blankets of trash in the air. London smogs, disaster at Donora, Pennsylvania, and dangers lurking over Los Angeles already accompany the buildup of pollutants in saucer-shaped city sites. Unrepentent urbanism tends to have it that nature no longer matters. However, nature now includes the products of our environmental misdemeanors.

Chapter 11

The Air Close Up

Attention has already been given to the urban atmosphere as a whole. But what about our more private atmospheres? In home and office, the personal climate becomes even more important (and more personal, if you consider respiratory gases). One person inhales and exhales some 0.4 to 4.0 cubic meters of air per hour (the amount depending upon level of activity, body size, age, and the like), partly used and loaded with water and other products of his own system. The volume of air in an ordinary living room may be around 100 meters or less. Breathing thus becomes a very intimate matter, modified of course by the amount of ventilation that is occurring. Even if we forget several potentially harmful gases, tobacco smoke contains some 10 million smoke particles per cubic centimeter. A room filled with cigarette smoke provides its users with a very polluted microenvironment. The upshot of this is that a city might succeed in controlling outdoor pollution only to lose the battle indoors, where most people spend most of their time.

We hear a lot about the dangers to health from air pollution. What are the destructive features of air pollution? The truth is that we need to know much more. We collect reliable and continuous statistics in only a few places. Statistics concerning causes of death are frequently open to question. Perhaps most of all we must take care not to confuse correlations with proved cause and effect relationships. Increased death rates may occur at times of high sulfur dioxide levels, but that alone does not prove that sulfur dioxide is the cause of death. Cadmium released into the air has been implicated in certain circulatory failures, yet it is not being routinely monitored everywhere. Lung infection of infants due to air pollution is reported. But is it due to airborne bacteria or to irritants that invite bacterial infections? We have counts on particles in the air but just what kinds do we have most to fear? Should we worry about industrial dusts, asbestos from brake linings and construction, particles worn from rubber tires, silica materials from many sources?

If asbestos is at all representative, we ought to worry a great deal. To begin with, it is difficult even to detect the presence of the extremely fine fibers in lung tissue, and only the immense powers of magnification of electron microscopes offer conclusive determination. It has long been known that asbestos means serious trouble for workers in various industries; but only now are we learning the modes of action of the tiny fibrils in the key organelles of lung cells. Yet a survey of New Yorkers' lungs showed that asbestos is commonly present. What will be the effects?

Other inorganic fibers are also collecting in our lung tissue. University of Pittsburgh investigators report that adult lungs carry from 15,000 to 400,000 fibers of all sorts per gram of tissue; they may constitute up to 6.1 percent of the weight of the lungs! The source of much of the inorganic fiber appears to be the ash of ordinary paper.

Many uncertainties, along with some uncomfortable general outlines, emerge. To what extent is lung cancer, now a very serious cause of death, one of enhanced interaction (synergism) of tobacco smoke with other things in the air that even non-smokers have to breathe? The evidence is now good that synergism is a principal phenomenon of air pollution. Hamsters, for example, are much more susceptible to bacterial pneumonia after having had contact with cigarette smoke and nitrogen dioxide than when exposed to either pollutant alone. Guinea pigs treated with sulfur dioxide in combination with manganese dioxide were less able to clear bacteria from the lungs than when either pollutant was administered alone.

Studies in Buffalo, New York, found that people with better incomes suffered less from air pollution than those with low incomes. All groups, however, showed increased death rates from respiratory diseases with increased air pollution. Similar correlation was found for cancers of the respiratory system.

In California, the incidence of respiratory-tract cancers almost doubled between 1950 and 1965. Such afflictions are three to four times as common in densely populated, smog-ridden counties.

Sulfur and nitrogen oxides are also implicated in gastrointestinal cancers. Recent studies suggest that concentrations as low as one-tenth of those which occur in large cities may increase the incidence of such cancers. Deaths from emphysema have apparently increased at the rate of about 12 percent per year for most of the last twenty years in California, and it is certain that air pollution is somehow involved.

Some more general figures: If all of Buffalo had air as clean as the cleanest parts (which is not exactly crystal-clear, and is well within the realm of the achievable), about 50 percent of the cases of bronchitis-related mortality could be eliminated. Urban death rates from pneumonia in urban England are 30 percent higher than in rural areas. Studies among white Americans indicate an incidence of lung cancer of 34 per 100,000 in rural areas, against 56 per 100,000 in cities of over 50,000 inhabitants. In Nashville, Tennessee, cancers of the stomach, esophagus, and bladder were 25 percent higher in areas with higher air pollution. In the same region, mortality from heart disease is 10 to 20 percent higher in urban areas. As a crippler, it is twice as high in urban areas. (Let us reemphasize that these are, at least as yet, only correlations; the exact role of air pollution is by no means settled.)

One of the automobile's chief atmospheric pollutants is carbon monoxide. A total of 100 million tons of this toxic substance is dumped annually into American air by autos, according to Resources for the Future, Inc. Even though recent evidence has underscored the dangers of carbon monoxide, it is far from certain that the most stringent controls envisioned will prevent its increase in city air. Although the Environmental Protection Agency has stipulated that nowhere should hourly concentrations of pollutants exceed 35 ppm, the concentrations of carbon monoxide in Los Angeles often reach up to 70 ppm for brief periods. Heavy traffic frequently creates carbon monoxide levels of 100 ppm, and traffic jams can cause levels as high as several hundred ppm. In the lungs of smokers, the concentration of carbon monoxide in the gases of the cigarette smoke may be on the order of 42,000 ppm. Yet it is becoming increasingly evident that even low amounts of carbon monoxide in the blood impair mental functions; 100 ppm causes dizziness; and 1,000 ppm, death. In auto-congested cities there is enough carbon monoxide in the air at times to reduce the blood's oxygen-carrying capacity by 20 percent.

Carbon monoxide is now carefully measured in many places. Lead content of the air is less fully recorded. We do know that during the 1960s lead content in the air increased by 60 percent in Los Angeles, 25 percent in Philadelphia, and 20 percent in Cincinnati. In the United States 20,000 tons of lead is released into the air each year. There are reports of a 300 percent increase of lead in the Greenland ice cap since 1940, another indication that the effects of urbanism do not stay at home. Rainfall at the La Jolla, California, station has shown lead concentrations ranging from 3 to over 300 micrograms per liter. The average is 40 micrograms per liter, which is only slightly above the average for a nationwide survey. The United States Public Health Service rejects as unfit for human consumption water with a lead concentration of 50 or more micrograms per liter. Almost all of this lead comes from combustion of leaded gasoline.

The Clean Air Act of 1967 and its amendments in 1970 and 1971 were aimed at control of carbon monoxide, particulates, sulfur oxides, hydrocarbons, and photochemical oxidants. Although 62 percent of the people polled in one survey suggested outlawing the internal-combustion engine (one of the major offenders in regard to particulates) by 1975, there is little likelihood that that will happen. The chances of real alternatives to the engine are even slimmer. Furthermore, it must be reemphasized that we do not know for sure what is killing us. Nor can we guess what will become more dangerous if we reduce one pollutant. So far, for example, most efforts at reducing factory carbon monoxide have increased considerably the amounts of dangerous nitrogen oxides.

There are many binds. Car ownership is strongly correlated with making cities bearable to many people. It is also certainly a symbol of economic and social status. Can you imagine a reversal in the trend toward urbanization, a lowering of average family incomes, or a change in attitudes great enough to reduce car numbers? Can we hope to develop and install a massive enough mass transit system to both serve peoples' needs and effectively displace automobiles? Part of the solution, of course, is to make cities nice places for people to live—and stay.

The deterioration of human health is a hideous enough aspect of air pollution. There are other facets to it. It has been known for many years that numerous species of plants are injured by such air pollutants as sulfur dioxide. Instead of taking that as a Distant Early Warning, we have cut the dead trunks and retorted that air pollution has not killed us yet. It has apparently killed some of us. Oxidants and hydrocarbons cause spinach to wither and have damaged crops of tobacco, beets, celery, and lettuce. Estimates of crop damage from California's smog vary from $30 million to $100 million a year. Lettuce and other leafy vegetables can no longer be grown successfully in Los Angeles County. Vineyards and orange groves around Los Angeles have had their production cut in half by smog. California produces about 40 percent of the table vegetables consumed in the whole United States. It cannot, therefore, be said that air pollution is merely a local or economic matter that is unrelated to man's immediate biological needs.

Man's modification of climate within or near cities is clear enough. Likewise, the amounts of wastes of a big city are not small. We dump sewage in a river, in the faith that it will somehow be purified enough to become somebody else's drinking water downstream. We expect air pollutants to be blown off and diluted into harmlessness in our common ocean of air. It is becoming increasingly clear that these things do not always happen.

Chapter 12

City Diseases in Man and Agriculture

There can be no doubt that the urban poor feel the crush of disease and purely urban afflictions more than the nonpoor. The Urban Coalition claimed in 1969 that the 25 million urban poor lose twice the number of days of work as the nonpoor. They spend much more time in bed sick. They suffer four to eight times the incidence of heart disease, arthritis, and other chronic conditions. Until such statistics are explained, it will hardly be possible to assign final causes to unnecessary urban deaths and suffering. A major mistake, however, would be to assume that it is simply a matter of money—or even that getting and spending more money is simple.

The politics of conservation is a complex matter. Consider how little we are apparently able to help the poor of today, with society more or less stable and services dependable. Think how helpless we might be in controlling a severe epidemic in such an urban area as New York City. While we tend to think all such outbreaks things of the past, we must remember that the great plagues of the past also burst in upon an unsuspecting world.

Imagine the invasion of a crowded and malnourished modern city by a new pathogen of great virulence. Suppose antibiotics were unavailable (as in underdeveloped countries) or only mildly effective (as with flu vaccines so far). What could prevent local disaster if, as with the great epidemics of the past, the water supply of a large city were colonized by a pathogen? (To get established, it perhaps only need be resistant to the usual, routine applications of chlorine.) It would hardly be necessary for everyone to die from it right away. The immobilization of social functions would spread to all levels of life. If operators could not work in electric generating plants, if drivers could not man oil delivery trucks . . . what then? Results might be more disastrous than anything except deliberate germ warfare or nuclear bombs.

Even with a relatively stable and healthy population, it was not possible for us to provide enough vaccine for the whole American population against Asian flu in the winter of 1968–1969. Thirty million Americans contracted the disease and 27,000 died from it. Information on such diseases and our tools for dealing with them come from the Center for Disease Control, a unit of the United States Public Health Service in Atlanta. What if an unexpected and virulent variety of flu happens to hit Atlanta especially hard? Production of the new vaccine for general marketing, at best, takes four or five months; at least a month must elapse after injection before it becomes effective. What happens if the highly centralized disease-control machinery itself is crippled? What happens if we do not know all the effects of all the types of influenza? Flu is serious business at best but there may be unexpected complications. Alberman and Fedrick examined 16,750 British children born during the first week of March in 1958, following a serious seige of Asian flu in England. Of the 14,791 mothers who had not contracted flu, only 6 gave birth to children who later developed leukemia. Of the 1,959 mothers who had had flu, 7 gave birth to children who later developed leukemia or related cancers. Flu, at least in this limited sample, seems related to a ninefold increase of leukemia, a burden if it turns out to be generally prevalent, that will be disproportionately borne by urbanites, for influenza is an urban disease.

And what about more resistant strains of pathogens? Several thousand cases of typhoid occurred in Mexico City and environs during the winter and spring of 1972. Street vendors and the water supply were blamed for its spread. One of the more disturbing points was that conventional antibacterials were not effective in curing victims. Ampicillin was, fortunately, found to work and the outbreak was contained. Such diseases as typhoid also make matters precarious because infected individuals incubate the disease ten to twenty days before clearly showing the symptoms. In the interim, they may travel great distances from the source of the disease and may infect many people. Some 2 to 5 percent of those contracting typhoid, furthermore, become carriers only; they never show symptoms of the disease but continue to spread it (hence the term "Typhoid Mary").

Many natural foci of the dreaded plague bacilli exist in the world today, including the United States. There have been cases in the United States, Israel, and Russia within recent years. What are chances that more virulent and more invasive strains will develop? We do not know what our proliferation of chemicals may do to produce mutations among water and soil organisms formerly not harmful (or harmful in minor ways) to us. (A 1970 survey revealed that 66 organic chemicals have been identified in freshwater throughout the world; some 430 others are suspected of being in the water because of their use in processes that produce wastewater.) It must be pointed out, however, that we know little about the capacity of pathogens for generating new and more deadly forms (or even whether any changes occurring will prove detrimental to man or not).

We do not know the exact sources of new diseases today (Asian flu being an example). A presumably new organism killed one-third of the population of Ireland in the years 1202 to 1204. The Black Death halved the number of people of Great Britain during the fourteenth century; London's 1665 plague resulted in 68,000 deaths. In these cases, new strains may have been involved. A hint as to how sudden the appearance of a new pathogen might be is shown by the fact that in 1967 a previously unknown (or unrecognized) virus struck down several workers in European laboratories. The Marburg virus, as it has been called, was carried by experimental monkeys; it readily escaped detection at airport inspections, proved frequently fatal to people, and was unresponsive to antibiotics (see *Science,* vol. 160, pp. 888, 1968).

In the United States in 1900, one-third of all deaths were due to infectious diseases. That incidence has been brought down dramatically but we hardly know the whole story. It would, for example, be interesting to know if we will in the future lose certain of our capacities to become immune to diseases. That the immune substances, produced by an organism to protect itself, may also themselves cause damaging or even fatal maladies (as reported upon recently by Notkins and Koprowski) adds a new dimension, as we move into a viral and bacterial One World.

Our recent success in dealing with infectious diseases has left us a little impatient of caution. But while the number of cases of diphtheria and polio have gone down sharply since the 1940s, thanks to vaccines, the number of cases of encephalitis is up. Infectious hepatitis has increased enormously, as have cases of streptococcal sore throat and scarlet fever.

In the absence of separate reports for death rates from diseases for rural versus urban areas, it is impossible to assess clearly the possible relationships between diseases and population densities as such. However, it is known that viral and bacterial diseases depending upon human contacts (as opposed to those spread by insects) are pretty much village and city diseases. Influenza rates are higher in the crowded East and North, as opposed to less crowded South and (especially) Mountain West. Various malignancies, as well as diseases of the heart, although not infectious, follow a similar pattern; one must suppose them related to urban air, water, food, and social stresses. (The milder and more stable climate of California perhaps accounts for a lower influenze rate there.)

However, among infectious diseases, it is not "normal" disease rates that we must chiefly worry about but the wildfire spread of epidemic diseases. New ones of this sort are presumed due either to changes in the human host, in the environment, or in the pathogen itself. The relative contributions of these three interacting factors are far from clear. Increasing densities and mobilities, as has been pointed out, increase incidence of contact. There may be changes in degree of infectiousness and life expectancy of pathogens after urban-induced changes in the physical environment occur.

Urban climatic changes may also affect the incidence of disease. Meteorologists note that cities are growing hotter and drier. In rooms, where we spend much of our time, humidity in winter may fall to less than 15 percent, a desert aridity that is detrimental to our noses, throats, and lungs (and apparently beneficial to influenza virus particles, which have been reported to be favored by dry air). The assault upon the respiratory system undoubtedly increases the susceptibility of people to microorganismal invasion, partly because of the general stress of changing temperatures and other conditions and partly because mucous membranes dry and become less effective in trapping and getting rid of suspended particles. There are complicated interactions here, for, with an increase in suspended particles in the urban air, the density and persistence of fog is increased. With increased fog, there is more bronchitis. There is also the possibility that droplet formation at the surfaces of bodies of water in sewage-treatment plants may pick up and toss into the air bacteria that swarm just below the surface of the water. Only a few of such bacteria are pathogenic, of course; but it is clear that we do not know the whole story of what is going on around us.

We are not, we must repeat, thinking about isolated dangers only. We are open to simultaneous assault. Our bodies may use up their capacities to withstand insults. They now fight off the effects of half a million and more artificial chemical substances that we have poured into the world. The case of the "sudden" appearance of mercury as a threat underscores the point. That we are tough is undeniable; but for that, it would be us, and not just brown pelicans and bald eagles, dying out from the effects of pesticides. But pesticides have not yet finished their run through the world ecosystem. Concentrating mechanisms within ecosystems may still turn them into our own worldwide and deadly enemies. And if not pesticides, will it be something else or some combination of substances considered harmless separately?

Finally, we are not isolated organisms in a laboratory test tube, even if we should wish it. A third of the population of Ireland starved or emigrated in 1845–1850, when disease rotted potatoes, their monocultural mainstay in a crowded, simplified ecosystem. A deadly disease among America's beef cattle would bring about more trouble than farmers' strikes or a transport breakdown. Cattle, like all agricultural animals and plants, are overcrowded, genetically weak, and ill-nourished individuals. When men are crowded and mobile, their diseases travel faster. So, under the same circumstances, do the diseases of domestic animals and plants. Wheat, the staff of life to much of the world's population, is hardly ever more than a step ahead of some obliterating fungus. Cattle have their hoof-and-mouth disease and many others. The worldwide trade among cities increases the likelihood that sooner or later each new disease, as well as the virulent old ones, of a plant or animal will be spread into every refuge.

Corn furnishes us with a timely example of the vulnerabilities which exist, and which we unwittingly make worse in some cases by our very sophistication and advanced technology. Aside from numerous insect enemies, corn is prey to various crippling diseases, some of them particularly characteristic of today's simplified ecosystems in agriculture—a simplicity that is biochemical, genetic, biotic, and economic. One aspect of this, vulnerability of key crops to disease because of genetic uniformity, is pertinently illustrated by southern corn leaf blight.

Hybrid corn is produced by growing two parental types in adjacent rows, usually six rows of the seed parent alternating with two rows of the pollen parent. Traditionally, the laborious process of hand removal of tassels of seed parent plants prevents self-fertilization. In an effort to lower the considerable costs involved in this part of seed production, Texas seed growers introduced a seed parent with a cytoplasmic factor that inhibited development of the tassel. This strain, assigned the name of Tcms

("Texas cytoplasmic male sterility"), soon dominated the market because of its lower production costs. At least it did until the summer of 1970.

The first inkling of trouble came in January in Florida, where ears and stalks of corn plants showed blight symptoms. Soon after, Alabama and Mississippi reported the blight. An unusually wet growing season (which, of course, would ordinarily have been considered favorable for the highly fertilized and closely planted crop) facilitated the wildfire spread of the disease. In July, fields in Illinois and Indiana began to turn brown, and ultimately much of the corn belt was affected to some extent by one of the most damaging plant epidemics in history. Losses exceeded by many times the destruction of food in the potato blight in Ireland in the 1840s. The average yield per farm declined 20 to 30 percent, and some farmers lost their entire crop. Nationwide, the epidemic cost $1 billion.

It soon became apparent that the blight had selectively attacked the Tcms variety of corn. The shift back to conventional hybrids depleted the supply of seed of the latter, and recovery by the next growing season was made possible only by a costly and well-organized program of growing seed corn over the winter in Florida, Hawaii, South and Central America, and the Caribbean. An extensive and effective educational plan, involving integrated cooperation among federal, state, and local governments; seed growers; and university research personnel, alone made the rescue possible. The press, too, had covered events thoroughly and there was widespread fear that the summer of 1971 would be a grim one for corn farmers. However, the summer came and with it little blight; conventional hybrids—and a drought in some of the key areas—helped to produce a near-record crop of 5.4 billion bushels (compared with 1970s 4.1 billion bushels).

The warning, often sounded by agronomists, is clear. Loss in genetic diversity in crop plants means trouble. If a disease had struck proportionally hard at the major food crop of a less affluent and still less diversified agriculture, the result would have meant loss of one-fifth of the crop—and hence widespread starvation. The United States National Research Council's committee on the genetic variability of plants offers little reassurance, even for American farmers: "Most major crops are impressively uniform and impressively vulnerable." Two bad years in a row (from whatever causes, of course) would wipe out most of our stored grain. It would also do much to erase our complacency about the future.

Chapter 13

Unwanted Sound

Noise is certainly a major stumbling block to enjoyment of urban life. Noise and its effects are hard to measure. People do object to it. The number of Europeans disturbed by sounds coming from outside the home more than doubled in the period 1948 to 1961. How do you evaluate peoples' feelings? Do you ignore complaints until people can prove they have suffered physical injury? And what kind of injuries do you recognize as "real"? It is estimated that the average factory worker, who is likely to make mistakes if he is unable to concentrate closely, may spend a fifth of his energy fighting off the effects of noise, and hence it is little wonder that bodily fatigue and noise exposure correlate. The efficiency of intellectual interchange, allegedly the major blessing of urban life, is lowered by noise. Psychic and physical damage may result. Noise, obviously, is not of small concern.

Why all the noise? Commercial planes of all types, with bigger and more powerful ones on the drawing boards, already cost millions in taxes and cause an untold amount of mental disturbance. Automotive vehicles of all types and sizes add their noises. To those add: private planes and helicopters, sirens, garbage trucks and trash cans, gasoline-powered lawnmowers, outside air conditioners, construction equipment of many sorts, household appliances galore, public address systems (including those intended to sooth our ruffled spirits), telephones, radios, television sets.

One of our last personal freedoms is being eroded. Once again, under the guise of up-grading our environment, we are selling for mere money and affluence what should be precious to us. As with many aspects of our polluted environment, if the body can stand the pollution for a fairly long period of time, we ignore the dangers. Physical measurements of psychical or long-term physical dangers just do not move us to appropriate action.

What can we do? A diesel truck can be somewhat toned down. Its 80 decibels of sound (as the human ear hears it) at 100 feet on the flat can be reduced to a much more acceptable 69 decibels if the roadway is dug in a trenchlike form below general ground level. (Remember that the decibel scale is geometric, and a smaller number indicates a very large reduction in the amount of sound heard.) Further reductions would result from building a noise shield along the road. But the total reduction gained from such methods will not keep up with the increases in horsepower, number of trucks, and size of loads that Progress demands for tomorrow.

We can fight back in other ways, of course. It makes no sense at all for us to tolerate a 50-horsepower motorcycle that makes as much noise (much of which could be muffled) as two 300-horsepower Cadillacs. We can also begin to act as if *all* places in which we live, work, or play are worth making comfortable: one downtown Boston school playground had an average sound level 100 times higher than the average level in Wellesley, a Boston surburb.

We can begin working for improvements almost anywhere. Modern engineers and architects have produced some of the noisiest buildings in existence. Lightness of materials, poor workmanship, poor insulation, and high rise elevations all contribute. In addition, at least 6 million American workers (and maybe as many as 16 million) are on jobs where noise, even by antiquated standards, is unsafe for the future of their hearing. Most-affected occupations include weapons testing and other Armed Services jobs; iron and steel making; motor vehicle production; textile manufacturing and paper making; metal products fabrication; printing; heavy construction; and mechanized farming. It is well known that people who live in quiet environments retain their hearing abilities much more completely than those who live in noisy surroundings. We know that noises equivalent to those of sonic booms, which accompany the passage overhead of supersonic aircraft, permanently damage the inner-ear sensory cells of experimental animals. So far, our most vigorous reactions to sonic booms have come because of structural and material damages to buildings and contents (no doubt because they are easier to prove legally than damages to the body).

Aside from hearing loss, noise may cause cardiovascular, glandular, respiratory, and neurological changes. These damages occur whether sounds are intense and sudden or of sustained high level. Cannot we develop better guides to safe exposure? Are we to say that induced deafness is just an occupational hazard that can be amply compensated for? In 1969, the British medical journal *Lancet* reported "a significantly higher incidence of mental illness requiring treatment among people most exposed to aircraft noise." Is this merely a marginal matter? Dr. Lester W. Sontag predicts that violent noise such as sonic booms may permanently damage unborn babies.

There are other aspects of sound that need exploring. Low-frequency sounds (so-called infrasonic sounds) travel over long distances without diminishing. They cause behavioral upsets. Perhaps the infrasonic waves produced by severe storm activities do the same thing. While it is not infrasonic, what are we to think of "white sound" (or "acoustical perfume"), a sort of broad-spectrum hum that is now being prescribed to smooth out "noise"?

In industry, people do lose their hearing. If they are alert (and lucky) they may collect legal damages. But noise levels encountered in the community often exceed those of factories. Live rock and roll music may at any time shatter your peace—and eventually your hearing abilities—with its 120- to 125-decibel noise level. Such noise is far noisier than most industrial jobs, and can destroy hearing as effectively as a jackhammer.

It is going to get worse. This applies to noise pollution, to water pollution, to air pollution, to congestion, to a myriad other frustrations. Each is being approached by different experts and agencies and thus, unlike the integrated response of the organism, the result is apt to be contradictory and counterproductive.

Part Four

Why Cities Grow Gray

Woe unto them that join house to house, that lay field to field, till there be no place, that they may be placed alone in the midst of the earth!

Isaiah, 5:8

It should never be forgotten that no privilege can be a right, and legislative bodies ought never to make a grant to a corporation, without express reservation of what many sound jurists now hold to be involved in the very nature of such grants, the power of revocation.

George Perkins Marsh
The Earth as Modified by Human Action

Chapter 14

Can We Plan?

Our failure to plan our cities in the past can only mean that most of us do not plan until events—for example, overpopulation—force us to do so. Is this real planning or just trying to keep up? And what about the planning, if it can be called that, that gets you in deeper? There is much of this going on today and it consists of assuming salvation from without.

In this regard, the United States sent 800,000 tons of grain a month to India in 1966. That was enough to feed some 40 million people. That number is about equal to the people subsisting in Indian seacoast cities. The city furnishes many desperately needy people there nothing they want except bare survival. They are not adjusted to impersonality and noxious assaults. They do not have the skills that one must have to command urban respect, let alone a job. Then cannot return to their places of origin for they remember them as offering no hope whatsoever. (Let us not cite other nations alone: the United States dependence upon Middle East oil and Peruvian proteins are pertinent examples.)

Can planning become something bigger than a working out of heartless economics? Can it not aid us in finding better priorities than those that have led us to barter away first natural beauty, and then clean water, and later good air? Planning can find ways to get us from cars to bikes, from bikes to mass transit. But can it show us the way from traffic jams to pleasant walkways and interesting things to see? Can it turn suburbs into something better than just ways to avoid the inner cities?

Power nourishes itself and leads to ever more power—until eventually it grows beyond even legislative control. The modern corporation is one such power center, and its activities, like money let out for interest and the growth of human populations, have a similar way of exploding geometrically. We cannot digest a diet of such uninterrupted expansion, even though many urban examples represent centralization of power and resources more than true growth. Why have we let such expansion continue until there are societies of people in circumstances so desperate that they have nothing to lose but their frustrations and constraints? Why do we allow nature to go unprotected until city-country contrasts (and the options that go with them) are obliterated by an urban saturation of pollution, waste, and greed?

One example of the tunnel vision of urban economics is the constant demands made upon remnant wilderness areas for such urban recreational uses as skiing. If cities need such areas (and it is obvious that they do), why haven't urban planners put this need into the equation that they use to describe other man-land relationships? Planners do not expect free industrial resources, highways, or airfields! They do not usually expect to acquire urban playgrounds for nothing. Such commodities have money value and they can be budgeted for accordingly. But when it comes to recreation that must be outside what is conventionally thought of as urban land (whether skiing, boating, hiking, or the like), wild-land natural resources are suddenly expected to cost little or nothing. Almost without exception, city planners look for slivers and remnants of wilderness habitat, often of high scenic and scientific value and very easily ruined. Nobody lives there; they are not intensively cultivated; their timber resources may be inaccessible or scrawny. Such hard-pressed land, noted for natural beauty and for the vigor with which it is defended by conservationists (whose claims are so easily dismissed in our society), suddenly interests planners and developers. Can we not find a way to plan for such necessary areas while nonurban land is cheap and plentiful?

If we really mean to plan for a high-quality life style for all people, we have to fit numbers to the resource. In this context, it is just as unfair to deny the sportsman his ski lodge as it is to deny a teenager a decent playground. Both might be classed as minority users and both must be integrated into viable urban economic planning. This, of course, means a broadening of the scope of urban economics far beyond what society is conventionally willing to pay for. What is more important is to recognize that, ecologically, a ski slope represents a tremendous geographical extension of the city. It extends what can only be called urban blight, even though it may be many miles from the home city that demands it. Concerned ecologists would like to be assured that users will not simply be the usual, thoughtless environment-be-hanged people who carve up the hinterland at the lowest possible cost to themselves. They must be responsible for the land—responsive to its needs, careful of its sustenance, and concerned about its future. And they must know its cost and be prepared to pay it.

A total of around 1 million acres of land a year is lost to urban demands. This is equivalent to an area somewhat larger than the state of Rhode Island. Of this, about 420,000 acres are covered with building sites and primary roadways. About the same amount is flooded by reservoirs, and an additional 160,000 acres are turned into rural roads and airports. Still more goes to rights-of-way for power lines. About half of the total is (or was!) agricultural land. Though large, these figures are small in relation to the total national area; however, they constitute a much greater proportion of the areas where most people live; that is to say, the impact of such changes as perceived in our day-to-day living is great.

Add to the undesirability of taking good farmland out of production the sprawl that results. Add to that the high cost of utility services and their inefficient and ill-coordinated operation.

Add the tremendous costs of adequate transportation, costs that occur whether you consider the environment or the individual and whether you plan for public or private transport.

Consider the unsightly and unhappy mix that is sure to result in destruction of good air, water, and views as both people and industries bid for use of the land. Is the market so sacred? If we can zone land to keep industry out of suburbia, cannot we zone to keep suburbia from becoming urban sprawl? Must a maximum return to developers be the major result of our laws and our economic system? Will our laws operate only to make exploitation easier or more orderly, and never operate to control us and our numbers?

Land prices in suburbs and cities are so high (frequently one-fifth or one fourth of new house cost) that people often cannot afford to build. But these prices bear little relation to the ecological value of land. In fact, they frequently bear little relation to the conventional economic value placed on land as such. Thus, although farm-land values only went up about 150 percent between 1946 and 1964, home lot prices increased over 300 percent. Who reaped the benefits from this increase? One study in California found San Francisco residential lots selling for $10,600 per acre in 1962, at a time when the average value of agricultural land was $408 (and intensive-use, irrigated land sold for an average of $2,301) per acre. A 1961 Illinois study found that the percentage of increase in selling cost of land converted to subdivision from bare field was 76 percent higher than the increase in all other costs—and the selling cost was 2,037 percent of the farm value of the land. Individual farmers can hardly be expected to resist temptations to sell under such circumstances. (Recall that there are frequently no laws to keep these lands from being sacrificed to development in defense against urban-level taxes, the latter being much higher than taxes on farm land.) But how long will we continue to sell irreplaceable agricultural land to the highest bidder, particularly land that is right where urban areas could derive the greatest benefit from it?

Chapter 15

Going Places?

Mobility is a myth. Man is the only encapsulated animal, and it is really only his various capsules that go places. We are born from one capsule and we are immediately encased in others. Our busy lives consist largely of hectic shifts from one restraining, cushioning capsule to another. Even our social roles are capsules: we escape from childhood's capsule into that of adolescence, from the latter into the capsule of adulthood and then of "senior citizen." We are encapsulated by the walls of our home, encapsulated at school. In capsules, of course, we go to the moon and into the depths of the ocean. What is most disturbing is that, in and by our capsules, we lose contact with and destroy the primary qualities of our natural environment.

The capsule automobile affects our primary environment through the by-products of combustion. Its rubber tires and asbestos brake linings are shredded into our air. Its lights and noises irritate us. Its roadways gobble up our land. The basic costs of road building are high, and maintenance expenses never end. Roads are slated and tarred, with noxious results. Herbicides used on roadway margins kill plants cheaply and indiscriminately.

Roads spin their ribbons of ecological influence across the country in every direction. They divide the countryside with what are, to some animals, impenetrable barriers of traffic, wire, and concrete. Their bridges form new links across deserts and large rivers (for some organisms).

We know something of the difficulties of disposing of a vehicle after it meets its end, usually long before it is really worn out, in a society of changing fashions and planned obsolescence. Roadways too suffer from untimely and costly abandonment—and for the same reasons.

The internal combustion engine, and particularly the automobile, is so much a part of the urban scene and so much a cause of urban collapse that it deserves this chapter of its own.

In 1972 there were a total of 112 million gas-powered vehicles in the United States. By 1980 there will be 138 million; by 1990, 162 million. Every time a baby is born in this country, two new automobiles are born. Total annual mileage jumped from 249.6 billion in 1940 to 788.7 billion in 1967, and total fuel consumption climbed from 16.3 billion gallons in 1940 to 65.6 billion gallons in 1970.

As if that were not bad enough, the rest of the world is catching the same fever. The United States share of world cars, trucks, and buses fell from 70 percent in 1950 to 48 percent in 1967. Can the world environment afford a population as extravagantly motorized as the small American population is?

The air we breathe shows the most immediate result of this. In 1966, automobiles were emitting as much as 80 percent of the pollutants assaulting the air we breathe.

Cars added 100 million tons of carbon monoxide to the air, mostly in cities. There now seems to be no level of carbon monoxide that is "safe." When carbon monoxide goes up, there is some addition to background carbonmonoxyhemoglobin in the blood and thus some impairment of the capacity of the blood to carry oxygen. One must not forget the relatively large amounts of carbon monoxide produced microclimatically by cigarette smoking.

Cars dumped 12 million tons of hydrocarbons, the diverse dangers of which we learn more about each day, into American air in 1966. There is now little doubt that both these and nitrogen oxides (6 million tons) are dangerous and expensive materials to disseminate into a world ill prepared to deal with them.

Cars also add about 1 million tons of sulfur oxides, which are damaging to vegetation, metal, stone, and most other materials, as well as irritating to man. They free 1 million tons of particulates, about 270,000 tons of which is lead. Half of the latter accumulates near streets and roads, with nearby soils and plants showing large buildups. The amount of floating lead particles in the air at San Diego has recently been increasing by 5 percent per year. That lead is extremely damaging to health no one doubts.

Thus our friend the automobile releases over 100 million tons of pollutants each year. And automobile pollution is by no means all we must contend with, although other air pollutors vary considerably as to what chemicals and what amounts they emit. In 1966 six major industries and all electric power generators produced a total of 43 million tons of pollutants. Space heating and refuse burning added another 13 million tons.

It can surprise nobody that such figures have meaning for human and environmental health. In 1970, the Philadelphia urban area released 700,000 tons of sulfur dioxide, 350,000 tons of nitrogen dioxide, 325,000 tons of hydrocarbons, and 650,000 tons of particulates into the air. That city experiences some degree of inversion (that is, periods when local weather keeps an area's pollutants at home) 200 days a year, and severe conditions constituting a health hazard develop 100 days a year. The latter situations are prime times for human health to be affected.

There are two major rallying cries by which one wins support for one's economic priorities: progress and jobs. If nature can be exploited, *progress* results. And nothing can be done to stop it, if conventional wisdom is to be believed. Once progress is under way, men earn salaries and nothing can be allowed to interfere with *jobs.*

Building roads is both progress and jobs.

The total United States mileage of auto roads (50 states) is 3.7 million miles, a figure that has steadily increased over the years. Yet the average number of miles of railroad devoted to passengers declined from about 106,000 in 1958 to about 60,000 in 1968. Intercity bus lines serviced very nearly the same number of miles, carried only a modestly increased number of customers, and made considerably less money in 1968 than in the mid-1960s. The United States remains a highly technological country where you cannot handily get by bus or train to any but our larger cities.

Highways are a critical part of America's economy. They also drain our land of resources of all sorts.

Roads are supposed to be a boon to our freedom and pleasure. A quarter of the population, however, cannot use them. They are also a congested and dangerous system that some of the rest of us use only because there is no alternative.

Roads may, indeed, take you to recreation areas. But they often impair nature's capacity to have something worth seeing at the end of the superhighway. They funnel too many people to too few scenic spots. They disrupt neighborhoods that might otherwise be pleasant, and foul the environment significantly along the way.

Total local, state, and federal highway spending is more than $17 billion per year, more than all these levels spend on housing, parks, recreation, sanitation, and fire and police protection combined. Other billions go for manufacture of vehicles, for repair, for fuel. Perhaps 15 percent of the nation's labor force is sustained by the highway and its closely related industries.

Thus the road interests benefit from an ever-increasing spiral of built-in subsidies and reinforcers. Roads must be built because they create jobs. Taxes paid by the users of roads go only to make new roads, whose building brings in more workers. The completion of roads confirms the need for new cars, which then need more roads before the concrete on the old ones has congealed.

Meanwhile, railroads rust and urban mass transit (where some 80 percent of the people could use it) proceeds at an oyster's pace. From 1947 through 1970, the United States government spent $58 billion for highways, $12.6 billion for airports and airline subsidies, $6 billion for waterways, and only $795 million, or 1 percent, for urban mass transit. Furthermore, federal money is assured (at a never-to-be-turned-down ratio of up to 9:1) long enough ahead of real commitment that it is possible to get funds to build a highway that has not yet been approved. At the same time, it may not be possible to obtain funds in much smaller amounts to build mass transit systems that have already been decided upon. Even amelioration, when that is allowed at all, is biased toward the highway interests.

Solutions to transport problems, out on the superhighway, are never far-reaching enough, and are soon swallowed in demands for more solutions. This is a pathological defiance of basic ecosystemic processes of self-control. In less profitable undertakings than national transport, it is sometimes noticed that people do not always want the things that they need to make themselves healthy. Is it not possible that fans of the automobile truly do not know what is good for them?

Only nonurban systems can effectively show up the deficiencies of modern urban life. Only real wilderness offers supreme examples of other approaches that we can study. Spiritual escape from today's urban condition is as necessary as that food be taken into the city. Escape can to some extent be symbolic, for some aspects of the wilderness model can be taken into the city. But escape must also to some extent be real. It is this that makes the failure of the automobile so personally hurtful to so many of us, for it does not succeed in delivering us from urbanism.

We would like to see at least 20 percent of the Highway Trust Fund (money collected as taxes on gasoline, automobiles, and related items) routed to the *reestablishment* of environmental qualities destroyed by highway and related construction. At least 10 percent of land in the United States presently buried under roads and buildings is no longer used for the purpose for which it was intended. It is now derelict, rotting real estate. We would like to see this land revitalized with natural plantings or agriculture. Create new jobs in the process. Raise challenging engineering problems of how to bring the diversity of the world back into the hearts and lives of large cities. Rooftop forests, new soil from waste materials, downtown vegetable gardens, and interior plantings like that of the Climatron in St. Louis are only a few of many exciting possibilities.

Chapter 16

The Dilution of Pollution

One of the products of urban metabolism is human sewage. Basically, it comes to some 100 gallons per person per day in American cities, 99.9 percent of it being water. Getting the water into the city is big business, and serious ecology. In getting the water, with its deceptively small percentage of true wastes, out of the city again, shortcuts have usually been taken. The results are ecological blows to our watersheds, and surface and underground waters and estuaries.

With tremendous expenditures and real devotion to the job, wastewater treatment could be made equal to the need for it. It will be a big task. About a third of the nation's population lives in areas where there are no sewers. Technically, they have no sewage problem. The other two-thirds burdens us with 1.8×10^{11} gallons of water annually, used to carry off wastes from homes, businesses, and industry. The relatively small part of this that is not plain water contains various solids, pathogenic bacteria, and such dissolved substances as phosphorus and nitrogen. Its organic materials swamp the bacterial helpers in inland waters. It also frequently contains DDT and other toxic materials which creep up food chains with disastrous results, and which can now be found all over the globe.

Of persons living in urban areas blessed with sewers, over 32 million misuse the sewers and dump their waste upon their downstream neighbors. They apply no treatment whatsoever, except to get the sewage out of their own sight and smell as soon as possible. In 1968, well over twice this number of people (82 million) had "adequate" sewage treatment, as judged by present standards set by government. Much of this treatment is questionably adequate. Some 32 million people treated their sewage in a way labeled by officials as less than adequate, usually just some sort of settling treatment.

In addition to all this, industrial wastewater is currently about 2.6 times that of domestic users. (Around half of the so-called domestic sewage is probably really industrial.) Not only are the amounts released large, but industrial effluent contains many waste products that are exceedingly hard to find out about and to remove. At this time, we do not even know if we have identified *all* the substances in industrial waste, much less those that tomorrow will be giving us trouble. Not long ago, no one worried about DDT. When we measured it at all, we ignored its accumulation in living tissue. Until relatively recently, detergents were claimed to be unmixed blessings. Phosphates were thought flatly good for ecosystems. Virtually nothing was known or done about mercury, cadmium, and much else.

Dispersion of pollution is no answer in a crowded world. One of the dangers of removing industry to the country will be to put off the time when even the most blind will have to see that something is wrong. By then, it may be too late to do anything about it. The whole business of water supply and water quality is not high enough on our priority lists, and our standards, such as they are, are almost entirely concerned with human health. Yet in the eastern seaboard region of Pennsylvania, Delaware, and New Jersey, 2.9 billion gallons of water were being used per day in the mid-1960s, and only an estimated 3.5 billion gallons per day are available. Normal economic maintenance in that region is now at stake, It is equally obvious that everybody will now have to pay for the sins of the past, whether he was individually guilty or not—and it will not be a one-time, lump payment.

The wastes of man are not all liquid. Domestic and industrial solid wastes, which cannot be flushed into the sewer, came to about 20 tons per person in 1972. This is expected to jump to 30 tons per person in 1980. About three-fourths of it was collected. Of garbage collected, the disposal varies: about 75 percent is dumped in the open, and about 15 percent is incinerated. Sanitary landfills capture less than 10 percent; a little is salvaged, and only about 1 percent is intentionally composted into useful fertilizer. The ecology of solid waste "disposal" is still in the Dark Ages.

Agricultural wastes are also a problem. The latter are, in a biological sense, as with much human sewage, not so much waste as simply overconcentrated or misplaced fertilizers. They are mainly plant remains, animal manures, and dead bodies. But a total of some 2.1 billion tons per year is produced. Much of this is unloaded near big urban centers and especially into rivers that furnish unfortunate people further downstream with their water supply.

Forestry wastes are also rather misnamed and, fortunately, are usually left in the forests. Mining wastes, although certainly wastes and certainly solid (1.1 billion tons per year), seem to occupy a different category from urban and industrial wastes. No one seems to doubt that we could, if we wanted to, frequently clean up after ourselves in mining.

Respiratory wastes are seldom publicly acknowledged, although always publicly shared. Garbage and solid wastes cannot be so easily concealed or ignored. Unfortunately, our society suffers an ecologically destructive blindness in regard to the organic remains that, as eating organisms, we reject and eject. We put all our emphasis upon eating and pay little attention to disposition of wastes, as if out of sight were out of mind. However, it is not that simple, even in matters of esthetics. Ancient Babylonians mixed their dung with mud to provide the strong walls of their houses. In arid zones, where wood is scarce, cooking still is often done over fires that burn loaves of cattle dung. In humid climates, human and animal wastes are not so easily disposed of. The glorious days of Athens were times of mountainous accumulations of manure, apparently not equaled again until the Industrial Revolution.

It would be a good idea for everybody to visit his sewage plant and his landfill—sanitary or otherwise—once each year. If he talks to city planners, he may be surprised to find that some of the land that one public servant means to use for agriculture another has tagged for landfill. Around large cities, the places available for the latter are already critically few, and not many cities can follow New York City's short-sighted practice of dumping its garbage into the sea. Inland cities frequently find their sewage returning to them in polluted groundwater. Landfills have a way of starting in low spots that eventually get filled in, following the city's tendency to smooth out all diversity of relief in the landscape.

One aspect of the proposed solutions to the waste disposal problem is representative of most modern urban thought in almost every field of endeavor—that is, shortsightedness. There is an overfocus on and overcapitalization of the centralized waste treatment plant. Even if people are content to live like feedlot steers, today's numbers of people make this solution unmanageable. The costs of building primary treatment plants for disposal of sewage in 1968 was about $148 per person for small groups of people (1,000 or less). An additional $175 per person would be required for secondary treatment (that is, providing for various aeration, filtration, and sedimentation processes that remove most—but not all—of the biologically active materials). For communities of 100,000 and up the costs are reduced to about $30 per person for primary treatment and $40 per person for secondary.

But still further treatments are going to be necessary if we really mean to have a clean environment. Furthermore, these figures do not include maintenance costs, nor do they take into account the enormously increased costs if more and more people spread out into suburban areas where installation and maintenance costs of additional miles of collecting pipes are involved. They say nothing about the hard fact that the bigger the collecting area, the bigger the disposal job—a disposal job that will finally overload some relatively small part of the environment. Neither is geographic dilution the answer. Individual septic systems will merely result in a rapid decline of environment everywhere, including the spread of nitrogen pollution and the dangers of contagion.

Another drawback to centralized treatment is that it allows citizens to become increasingly irresponsible in regard to what they dump into public waters, just as cities are irresponsible about what they dump downstream. If a city dumped its sewage effluent upstream, it might see the reasons for proper treatment before release. Using somewhat similar logic, we propose that apartments and houses have individual recycling plants. The salvaged products of such recyclers would be useful: freshwater, minerals, metal, paper, and the like; wastes would remain where they originated, in innocuous form. Everyone would try to get maximum value from his own water. With so intimate a knowledge of what they were drinking and turning over to agriculture and factories, citizens would be more careful about what and how much they put into the system.

Chapter 17

The Search for Community

Why have people been so attracted to the city? Some claim that the city offers greater freedom. That is hard to see. To an ecologist, freedom is almost an environmental constant proportional to the number of species present. The more kinds of things living in a particular place, the greater the potential for interaction with them, and hence the greater the potential for human and other life. One species may provide an aromatic oil, the next fuel for fire, the next clothing, the next inspiration. The loss of any one species means the diminishing of man as a species—and of the world forever.

In any case, the freedom a particular area offers must be divided among those who live there. There is only so much to go around. More people per unit area means less freedom per person, since people must compete with others for the world they occupy. Freedom in this sense is minimal in the city. But man is adaptable. Most people accommodate to the city, especially if they are born there and know little else useful for comparison.

Some claim that one gains freedom through the anonymity a city can provide. But surely life, full life, is never found in being aloof, apart, or uninvolved. Full life is experience, challenge, and accomplishment. It is diversity and reflection upon encounter. It is not entrapment within anonymity. To us, as ecologists, anonymity means social parasitism and irresponsibility. It means the college professor who spends his life at a chain of three-year stints at a series of institutuions, never participating in the life of the host society, rarely if ever understanding the business and political life of the (to him) faceless people who provide the structure for his day-to-day existence. Anonymity is the life of the working woman in a downtown metropolis who spends her days focused on a single task and almost never plays a role in shaping the scene spread out before her. Well-adapted people rarely come to the city *for* its anonymity, although once there, they are frequently consumed by it.

Some say that the city has culture. It is there that you find the plays, the great museums, the art galleries, the symphony orchestras, the baseball teams, the dramatic examples of architecture, engineering, and science. But, we say, is that enough? Is it reasonable to replace all the dog-tooth violets with a single Lincoln Center, the brooks with the gleaming white way of Madison Avenue, the sparkling air of a sea beach with the drama of the Manhattan waterfront? Most of us want all these things, want everything we can enjoy to be available. Unfortunately, the city all too often replaces one with the other, rather than adding one to the other.

It is doubtful, however, if either irrational yearnings or rational choices entirely determine our tendency toward living in cities.

Cities and city-dominated political states enjoy inflated power because of their superior science and technology. They exercise the enormous centralized power gained from the delegation, and loss, of power by the masses of people. But individual needs and goals of most people are not necessarily well served by such a system. The purposes of the state, and of certain persons in it, become more and more out of touch with the people. State power then manifests itself in war: both war against nature and war against other states of power.

The people-resource bases used to attract and make available large amounts of delegated power and wealth must also be large. Villages will not do so well as big cities. Cities are thus popular with the so-called leaders of men. In our own day, desire for princely power has been replaced by a hope for general affluence. Making everybody a real king seems never to have been a sociologically successful venture. Making everybody affluent may not be an ecologically valid answer, either.

The city is an abstract and extracting economy whose popular symbols are often far removed from actual resources. It serves extremely well certain parts of each of us, such as our desires for the sensual and the extreme. The needs for balance, or a kinship with nature, are not so well served. Such abstraction as is common in cities allows ready accumulation; the fact that money, stocks and bonds are prime symbols of wealth is a good example. Concentration encourages abuse.

To only a small number of even the leaders in cities will philosophy and creativity be of major concern. These qualities are important to many of us, but they are not guaranteed by the mere shell of a city! We may lose the ability to cultivate them in cities if we forget that cities must serve a broadly social purpose.

But what is wrong is not city building so much as that a variety of alternatives is not being kept alive. Streams and creeks are being culverted over. Such burial of the living is hard to stop. At Union College, where one of us teaches, there is a lovely brook which ambles through a garden, a garden visited in their day by Audubon, John Burroughs, and others. The stream is a primary image in the school's song. Still, plans are underway to culvert much of it over to accommodate an enlarged field house. We lecture against such activity a few hundred feet away, even while boiler-water wastes from the school powerhouse, with many chemicals in solution, are poured into the same stream. We are told that the actions are economical. We retort that blindness and weakness are additional reasons for the events.

Cities continue to grow. Forests that have taken hundreds or thousands of years to grow are swept away. Soil is smothered under asphalt. The water table is starved of pure precipitation or injected with the by-products of industrial and residential abuse. Air circulation and sunlight are shut out or altered. In short, almost every basic resource feature is being committed to a narrow, specific use that leaves us negligible maneuverability for the future. By design and by default we are destroying village and rural communities. Yet it is from those varied communities that some of man's future vitality is sure to spring. It is against that social hinterland, to some extent, that urban environments will be measured and urban achievements viewed.

The modern cosmopolitan city is a parasite, even if a lovely one at times. Why are we so far from building cities that serve the purposes envisioned by the true cosmopolitan? Our urban areas are centers of ecological overloading by heat, toxins, trash, people, and rotting housing. They are centers of overtransport of food and materials. That they may also be centers of misuse of finite material riches and undeveloped mental potential is something we need to think about.

Some will have it that the city and country exist in harmony, each contributing to the general well-being of society. But that is not so, at least not in our day and country. Cities are great magnets for every conceivable resource. They convert these resources into wastewater and paper, garbage, abandoned cars, stoves, refrigerators, mattresses, other household goods, and unabated air pollutants. Most of all they produce more than enough people who demand ever more resources or unhappy people who want to live in the country. The cities also serve as media centers which generate ecologically unsound needs and greeds across the countryside.

The city will always represent, even when ideal, a tight interplay between beauty and a supreme threat to all beauty. From it will eternally come the sneer "What good are dodos?" The guttersnipe illusion began with Socrates, who thought that the stars, stones, and trees had nothing to teach *him*. But it did not end with him. Saint Augustine's City of God looks distressingly like the autocratic shells that modern cities have usually become. And Hegel brashly said that only the modern city offered the mind its proper surroundings. "We are thus," retorted Albert Camus, "living in the period of big cities. Deliberately, the world has been amputated of all that constitutes its permanence: nature, the sea, hilltops, evening meditation."

Hegel might be right if we could produce a city that were in organic balance with nonurban regions, and not just an earth-bound place with oversize buildings and a traffic problem. Unhappily, Camus is right if you look at what cities usually do to the world that gives them life.

Chapter 18

People Pressure

One of the most ominous threats to the environment lies in the failure of man thus far to provide humane solutions to the problems posed by the spread of his own numbers. No major urban center in the world has yet demonstrated satisfactory ways to accommodate growth.

The President's Council on Recreation and Natural Beauty, 1968
From Sea to Shining Sea

Most Americans live in cities. People who lived on farms in the United States in 1960 numbered about 16.6 million, 2.5 million (15 percent) of whom were nonwhite. In 1968, an estimated 10.4 million people lived on farms, some 363,000 fewer than just one year before. The farms' losses were the urban areas' gains, a fact that was briefly noted in Chapter 1. The shift, in addition to being obvious, was also selective. By 1967, nonwhite farm residents numbered 1.2 million, only about 11 percent of the total farm population or some 4 percent less of the total than in 1960.

And the cities got bigger in complex ways. It was much less organized growth than chaotic sprawl. Of the 132 cities of 100,000 or greater population in the United States in 1960, 42 had had a population decline in the previous decade. [Lest this sound impossible, it must be noted that the declines were in city centers. The inner cities as a whole grew only about 1 percent during the period of 1960 to 1968, although their surburban rings grew by about 25 percent.]

Population changes were complex and biased. Black populations in United States cities grew by 2.6 million between 1960 and 1969; white city populations declined by 2.1 million in the same period. In 1967, out of an estimated population of 195.7 million, some 26.1 million (13.4 percent) had poverty-level incomes by United States Labor Department standards. Children under 16 made up 40 percent of these poverty-stricken people, and it is clear that they will change their status only with difficulty. White poverty-level persons made up 10.3 percent of the white population, while poverty-level nonwhites made up 35.4 percent of their group. (Although it can hardly be held that children were an economic blessing to them, the poor people cannot be blamed for the baby boom: by 1970, about 32 percent of the babies born came to poor and near-poor families; 68 percent of them were born to nonpoor Americans.)

But the poor, like children, consume taxes. In addition to the well-advertised burden of arms expenditures, these are aspects of taxation usually ignored. If the affluent are to give their own children and the children of the nation the presumed benefits of schools and other social services that their numbers demand, there is further reason for pessimism. Our 1 percent population growth already absorbs about 4 percent of our national income, some $30 billion a year. It is hard to see how that can continue without some serious squeezes felt by someone. It is already being felt by the aged and by the urban and nonurban poor.

Still, the common response of most city fathers is to "build up the tax base." The hope is to garner more funds for the maintenance of existing facilities and for the construction of still more. There is talk of attracting industry to pay the taxes, although the people who serve industries are also tax spenders.

Surburban development, the ultimate umbrella, is also held to be good. Home owners pay more taxes than apartment dwellers and thus they are thought more valuable members of the community. But they expect better service, better utilities, better schools, better roads, better police protection (or perhaps we could read "bigger" in all these categories). What happens, of course, is that city officials exchange the future of the community for the solution of small problems in the here and now.

Even if the desired growth occurs, what does a city do when taxable industry grows old and fails, to be replaced by block after block of derelict structures disfiguring the land? Who wants to pay to raze a tired old building? What businessman is interested in putting a new building in unpleasant surroundings? There used to be alternatives, when the land was rich in resources of coal, timber, hydroelectric power, fine agricultural land—and space and time. But not today. Much of our capital has been used up and we have not learned to live within our income. Is it not possible that one of the first lessons we must learn is to provide Earth with a more optimal sized population?

It turns out that using cities as dumping grounds for surplus people is not a very good answer, for either city or hinterland. The reasons are many, but in California's largest city as K. F. Watt explains, local taxes cost each person about 50 percent more than in small cities of less than 100,000 population. Public works expenditures are some 28 percent higher per capita. Police protection costs about 57 percent more per capita in large cities, which is high even taking into account the city high crime rates. Land also costs (that is, sells for) more. Since land sells for more, the tax structure begins to favor urbanization of farmland. Then it costs more for people to live in the country, and it costs everyone more when they move to town. Furthermore, asphalt produces no cabbage, as we have already pointed out. With 43 percent of the vegetables produced in the United States coming from California, the rush to turn good land into cities affects the welfare of urbanites everywhere.

Chapter 19

Density and Sanity

Are people misfits in cities? Perhaps it is cities that make them misfits. Storable surplus was the success story of the agricultural revolution and cities thrived on that. How long can cities stand being the dumping grounds for the surplus people generated by our highly technical, automated agriculture? People now go to the cities not because of an assurance of plenty or because of enhancement of opportunities. There is no other place for them to go.

The needs of people in urban masses are real enough. So far, those needs have been ill-served by most of the techniques for "bettering" the lives of individuals. Selling people more gadgets, for example, may not help them much; gadgets carry little meaning for individuals at psychological, social, and ecological levels. Will lip-service to the one-man, one-vote concept, or perpetual institutionalized education, or endless spectatorship for all "better" our lives?

What must we do? Will we be like the later Greek cities, rich in physical science and governmental structures but poor in bringing out the best in people? Remember that even the so-called Golden Age Greeks did not correspondingly elevate women, slaves, and merchants. Will our greatness and the benefits of our civilization also lack relevance for the majority of our people?

We already have little control over the quality of what we buy and sell. The failure to care (which seems inevitable in our system) is the final blow to humane society. People do not forget to care; they learn to avoid caring in order to reduce pressures of interaction and interdependency. Since it is impossible to interact warmly and sincerely with a thousand people a day, crowded people devise ways of remaining alone in crowds. The unfocused eye, the blank facial expression in the subway, the avoidance of the next-door neighbor, the ability to tolerate remarkable physical contacts without reaction—these are a few of the techniques the city dweller uses to be "alone."

Caring also requires roots. It is good business and good military technique to keep a man and his family from becoming rooted in the local community by shifting him frequently from place to place. Some people choose this mobile life style (at least for a while) because it gives them the freedom of anonymity; they have no allegiances or responsibilities to social causes greater than the employing institution. Thus cities become giant transportation depots, with people on the move from apartment to apartment, suburb to suburb, city to city. In contrast, the man responsible for the soil is attuned to rhythms, seasons, and cycles that form him and the animals, plants, and men of his acquaintance into an organic whole.

The Crowded World

About two-thirds of our people now live on 9 percent of our land. On this 9 percent, the average density of population is over 400 persons per square mile. It is, of course, much higher in the large metropolitan areas. But there is, you will say, all that land out there for cities to expand into. Is there? Cities have to gather resources from far beyond their borders. Lettuce from California, fish meal from Peru, tea from Burma. And that is only part of the story.

In 1960 the average density for the whole country, including Alaska and Hawaii, was 50.6 persons per square mile of land area. It is now about 60 persons per square mile. This means that each person has only about 10 acres of ice-free, reasonably habitable land today for all his needs and wants: food, homes and roads, airports, places to grow trees and raise cattle, national parks, ski slopes, and lands for wildlife. (World averages are about the same; so there is no empty land out there either unless you can persuade someone to surrender his share.)

And on that 10 acres each person must find room for his descendants and for all the land that they will require. In the forty-eight continental states, about 103 million acres was occupied by urban structures, intensive recreation areas, transportation, reservoirs, and the like in 1960. It has been estimated that by the year 2000 the area so occupied will total something like 229 million acres. Much of the land that will be so used is now prime agricultural land, and its loss will be felt.

If present trends continue, there will be twice as many people in the world by the year 2000 as there are now. If you think that the average of 5 acres of ice-free land that will then be available (on the average) is a lot, remember both what then will have to come from it and that land now is very unequally divided among the people of the world. You can expect to find that a very crowded 5 acres!

The Burdened Mind

Stress results when resources, in the widest sense, are too few or overused. In the Midtown Manhattan Study, conducted by the Cornell University Medical School, a sample of residents living in an area with a density of 600 persons per acre showed various indicators of desperation. (See Leo Srole et al., *Mental Health in the Metropolis,* 1962.) The subjects showed very high rates of alcoholism, suicide, accidental death, juvenile delinquency, and tuberculosis. In their noisy, demanding, crowded world, 20 percent of them were severely mentally incapacitated and only 20 percent were free of symptoms of mental disease. Yet, in a narrowly biological sense, those people had adapted to the demands of their world. But that people indistinguishable from inmates of mental hospitals are "adapted" is a grim commentary on what we are willing to do to ourselves.

Can the mind bear the burden of its creations? We do not always act as if we cared.

Pressure is not entirely psychological. There are too many dependents. There are too many youngsters entering the labor market all at once. There is not much room for them in unskilled jobs anyway. The numbers of these nonproductive persons increase as long as populations grow as they do now. Women are threats to mens' jobs and status—and vice-versa. New housing is costly and inadequate. Schools are crowded.

Society is polarized along lines of age. Within the system we have built, the young hate the old for many reasons, and old have ample reason for hating the young. The aged will make up an increased percentage of our population when and if we ever achieve effective control of our numbers (although the proportion will not be as bad as propagandists for reproductive irresponsibility often claim, and, with fewer children to pay for, society may at last be able to provide adequately for the old).

Care of the old is now a disgrace to the nation. Hatred usually results from apartheid. The role and value of age is lost to the young and the memory and delights of youth are forgotten by the aged. Society is the worse for it. Consider the number of elderly men and women who now live alone in large and encumbering houses while many in the nation go without adequate housing. Think of the educational loss to the young when the experienced are shoved aside upon their retirement. The age classes of our society have lost the means to interact, and a major factor in this transformation has been the crowded, competitive, and deficient environment of the city.

These conditions, plus many others, contribute to the "coldness" of social structures in big cities. It is after all, impossible to interact with all of the potential 220,000 individuals you can meet in Manhattan, and you must certainly exclude at least 219,000.

You not only have no time for pleasantries. You cannot even trust very many of them. That is not entirely because they do not know you. Some of them are dangerous because they are sick, enraged, and imprisoned without hope.

Do we want to encourage a system that confines most people to undesired (or undesirable) living conditions, so that a few thousand people can enjoy the rewards of contacts with, at most, a few hundred persons? This is a difficult question to ask, answer, or gather facts about. What drives one man insane is "exciting" to another. So far, we have not been notably successful even in persuading the speed kings that streets are for people.

The pressures that both the enjoyers and the haters of afternoon traffic undergo are hard to measure. Using blood pressure as a measure, it is known that both are under great stress. Many people work under stress too. But in the work place, high blood pressure is characteristic of people who have not yet made the grade. Those who are on top and those who know they are not going to make it to the top are less stressed. Stress is not merely upon circulatory systems. A study in New Haven suggests that schizophrenia and psychoneurosis are more plentiful among people who have advanced far and rapidly through the ranks from lower stations. This may be similar to the mental stress under which migrants operate. A New York study showed mental illness among migrants to the city from less urbanized areas of America to be higher (up to 300 percent greater than for "natives") than for immigrants born in foreign countries.

Clinically (and subclinically, for many people exist for years on their weekly visits to doctors who can find nothing wrong with them) there may be no cure for some. For others, it is appropriate to ask why they behave as they do, and whether their behavior can be changed. A wide range of opinions has it that better cities will make better citizens. If this is true, how may we look for ways to do a better job of city making? It might be worthwhile to find out how and why some people adjust to urban, even unpleasant urban, life. A dull-witted person may fit in easily. Someone else may do so only by coming to ignore such stimuli as the sight of people in need, or the high city noise levels.

It is, at any rate, time to stop saying that people are untouched by the social worlds they live in. Their circulatory systems break down. Their minds snap. One reason that city environments are so popular, of course, is because of the presence of a few intensely exhilarating experiences. But consider the findings of John B. Calhoun in a study of crowded rat and mouse colonies. The animals there certainly respond to their environments! Their intense sociality led Calhoun to coin the term "pathological togetherness" to describe the way they run themselves to destruction. Irregularities in feeding, breeding, infant care, periods of activity, territoriality, general mobility, and other behavior become rampant. Some individuals may reproduce themselves, but the colony as a whole soon fails to do so. Deviant social behavior and fighting are especially common among the lower ranks but at the bottom are a mass of individuals who *do nothing.* They may not even defend themselves.

We use test mammals to see if medicines will help or harm us. We mislead only ourselves if we do not take advantage of studies on animal behavior too. It is especially misleading to claim that while rats in laboratories cannot move, *we* can. Tell that to the residents of Harlem or Watts. In an increasingly crowded world, all of us will have fewer choices. Present unrest may be our species' way of responding to population pressures. It would, however, be extremely unwise to expect this to yield a lowering of population until organized society breaks down. We can learn from rats but we are not rats. They suffer little from a breakdown of their society. We shall suffer much. With each deterioration in the ecosystem, in addition, our choices are further limited. Soon there will be no place to hide, psychologically or physically.

Urbanism against the Wall

One of our major enemies may be our notion that you can patch up society with paper tape. Take, for example, one of the things that people do to themselves to make city life livable. New York City alone has about 100,000 heroin addicts. More than 900 fatalities due to drugs occurred in that city in 1969. Drug abuse is the leading cause of death among people of ages fifteen to thirty-five. (This includes drug-related allergic reaction, overdose, and needle hepatitis.) There are altogether some 200,000 drug addicts in the nation. Their drugs cost them something like $5 billion a year.

You can call this social breakdown. You may prefer to say that it is cyclical alternation of conservatism and permissiveness in social mores. But drug addiction typifies the big, big city. So does a high gonorrhea rate. Figures for gonorrhea for Los Angeles county indicate a rate of 333 per 100,000. In areas within the county in which the socioeconomic level is low, rates run from about 800 to 2,500 per 100,000.

So much for what people do to themselves. Consider those who strike out at society in general. Between 1960 and 1969 the population increased by about 13 percent, and one's chances of being the victim of crime more than doubled. And the risk was not evenly distributed. The occurrence of murder in cities of over 250,000 in 1972 was 19.7 per 100,000; in the suburbs, the rate was 4.6 and in rural areas, 7.4. Burglary, as an example of crime against property, occurred in the cities at a rate of 1,878 per 100,000 inhabitants. In suburban areas, the rate was 963 and in rural areas, 507. (Data are from the FBI's "Uniform Crime Reports" for 1972; Washington D.C., August 1973.)

It is possible that violence is more closely tied to density per se than has been generally believed. Considering murders in rates per 100,000 of population, R. L. Kyllonen (1967) has classified American cities by size, from class I (250,000 and over) to class VI (under 10,000). For these six classes, he calculated murder rates of 6.8, 5.6, 3.3, 2.9, 2.4, and 2.7. He found population density more important in determining murder rates than unemployment, family disturbance, and mental disorders.

It can be pointed out that not all big cities of the world show such evidences of stress and responses to stress as these. About the only moral we can extract from that smug rejoinder is that things do not have to be as bad as they are in American cities. Beyond that, a prudent person would observe that real urbanization is only now hitting its stride in vast areas of the non-American world.

Chapter 20

New Names, Old Problems

Some systems analysts (or cyberneticists) think of societies in big cities as "urbanized systems." They suggest that these systems show goal-seeking qualities; that is, they "sense" their condition and then modify their behavior. If this is true, where do the snags begin?

E. S. Savas of the New York City government thinks, first of all, that the tenures in office of elected officials and the real times required to accomplish much do not coincide. Mayors come and go; but it may take at least a human generation for a particular group of people to acquire and apply a harmonious life style.

Technical lags occur too. Good data on emphysema rates seem to be four years old by the time we can collect and begin to act upon them. It took us a long time to begin to worry about DDT. Good quality urban mass transit, even though we need it badly, is still not off the drawing boards. It appears that as economies become more highly technological, shifts of strategy cost more money and require longer lead times for accomplishment.

The machinery of government is frequently very cumbersome. One answer is to decentralize certain so-called "minor loops" of the whole system, such as schools. This allegedly frees the central government for more important matters. But it frees the minor loop, too, and trouble erupts when the local group rebels and refuses to accept the usual standards. Unexpected behavior may occur, stumping the experts. For example, job training, job creation, and low-cost housing might be expected to decrease the number of unemployed and slow down deterioration of homes. In fact, it sometimes does just the opposite. There are today a great many qualified workers waiting for their kind of jobs while on relief. In a very real sense, then, training has created the unemployed. Residents of St. Louis are well aware of their contribution to low-cost housing in the Pruitt-Igoe project, recently demolished as a public liability. Similarly, the massive bureaucratic machinery that is supposed to protect the city from being cheated may bring in bids only from the higher bidders; the people who could save the city money may simply not bother to fight the mass of red tape.

Two very serious nubs of trouble plague city systems. First, problems not recognized as trouble spots by the public (such as the need for birth control many years before overpopulation occurs) will never be tackled by officials who must depend on popular support for their election. Programs simply never get funded or they do not start early enough to accomplish anything. Second, a particular program's success or failure is often the result of unpredictable factors. New York State's medicaid program succeeded better than experts had expected (more people applied than had been supposed would bother), and it had to be cut back. On the other hand, although a good deal is known and has been made public about relationships between smoking and lung cancer, nearly 50 million people in this country aged seventeen and over fail to heed the warning. The demand for law and order even though costly, may persist despite taxpayers' rebellions about the high cost of schooling.

It is not, then, simply a matter of assuring the election of politicians who have caught up with the facts of life. Such officials cannot revise our priorities unless we listen to them. Still, it would be good to have more leaders in politics and industry who habitually did not deny unpleasant truths. They all too frequently reinforce our beliefs that, by a little further despoliation of a beautiful world, we can extend our dominion.

It is not easy to present a catalog of rules for living in the city or for making a satisfactory city. Our last chapters will be largely concerned with just these matters. We know that what we do not need are eternal innovation and fitful change. We have plenty of that and it turns all of last year's rages into this year's cliches. It results in a worship of either the untried or the trivial. It results in a worship of the young—at least, of the young in purse. It is no sin to be young, but why must people past middle age be stigmatized as hardly human? Currently, we act as if it would be better to find some secret of eternal youth than to find decent lives for old people. But the results of this way of thinking have begun to be reflected in a lowering of the quality of life of our whole society, young as well as old. We seem to have valued the city more as a place for mindless activity than for its human contacts. Do urbanites want something or do they simply want to escape from something?

It seems improbable that we can have a great city unless we hope to make something of lasting human value at the same time. The tying of the city to a translation of man as solely an economic being is unfortunate. Man has many motivations besides the economic. Some of them are not particularly lovely. They do, however, enable us to see that high civilization sometimes consists of controlling ourselves. Man is not an angel led astray by the evils of society.

We had better try to find ways to live with ourselves. The time is past when we can hope to leave our troubles behind us by inventing better means of transport. And the time has come when the rest of nature cannot tolerate our transgressions.

Chapter 21

Why Have We Lost Ground?

Cities and urbanization direct people away from ecological reality. The world of the urbanite jangles with electronic devices; it is made worrisome by thousands of manufactured objects. Much that is not shabby is vicarious and empty. It is the world of spectator sports. It is all real, of course, but it has led us to deny nature and the teachings of nature, as the term nature used to be understood.

Urban skies are several tones of blue lighter than those of rural regions. But to whom do you appeal for bluer skies? Shall we add to myopia a prescription of colorblindness as a quality best fitting man for the city? We do not think so. Our reasons are hard and objective enough, but they come from that nonhuman nature that the urbanite majority now knows so poorly. Still, there seems some hope that current interest in the ecological breakdowns that we have caused (air pollution is an example) may lead us outward to see what nature has to teach.

Meanwhile, we probably run the risk of being called silly utopians, even though the dreaming of utopias is not our aim. What has happened is that all of us know so little about homemaking on a real earth that to get anywhere near the truth is to skirt the utopian. The aim here, however, is to discuss ecological reality as a model and not to defend preconceived, man-centered ideals that have led us into so many dilemmas.

We are in the dilemma of Bulkington, in Herman Melville's *Moby Dick:* "The port fain would give succour; the port is pitiful, in the port is safety, comfort, hearthstone, supper, warm blankets, friends, all that's kind to our mortalities. But in that gale, the port, the land, is that ship's direst jeopardy."

Are we really learning anything? Or will we keep right on reusing theories that have proved baseless? Do architects go back to and reflect upon their paragons of individual creativity, with their skillful use of architectural achievements and their perfections of insight? Or are changes taking place too fast for that to be useful even if they did?

It is easy to laugh at the ideals of people who want to get us out of our present mess. The trouble with making fun of ideals (and some of them are pretty vulnerable) is that our society is itself powered by a host of ideals that never get examined objectively. Progress, as presently conceived, for example, is not really perpetually possible. Technology may not be able to correct its own mistakes. More gadgets do not guarantee happiness. The market place is not more important than religion or education. The misguided individual ego may not be a fair judge of ecological responsibility. The new is not always better than the old.

Such attitudes hardly qualify as ideals in the usual sense, but they are the driving forces in our society. A good many commentators and citizens are as savage with backpackers, bikers, and birdwatchers as with despoilers. The upshot of it is that if you eliminate only the very worst of the spoilers, the great dedicated majority (most of us) goes right on as before. If you eliminate the backpackers (and the seers, naturalists, and poets), on the other hand, you stop at the fountainhead any hopes we have of getting new, uncluttered views of man and nature.

Ecologically uninformed notions get us in deeper. Take the view that air and water are free, or very cheap. The truth is that they have simply been outside the realm of our economic theories. The result has been that our value system let them be used as subsidies for exploitation of those things upon which a price could be put. While exploiters, such as men of the now-defunct Monterrey sardine fishery or the lumbermen who gutted redwood forests, raided our environment of recognized treasures, they also deprived it of clean air and good water. Thus, the total cost of living went up; and it always went up much faster, in ecological terms, than the economic "growth" that caused the damages.

We are often told that American manufactured goods and services cost little. Compare cotton yard goods with handcrafted fabrics, for example. But if you examine the quality, the goods are usually cheap in more ways than one. Does the price tag tell the whole story? Remember that we pay for them not only the price at the store but also the resources that constitute them and the pollution of our environment. It is a peculiar set of ideals that leads defenders of the system to claim suddenly that we must be willing to pay for clean air. So we must. But so must they. It is time that exploiters (perhaps this means all of us in some cases) learn that one of the payments must be in not polluting in the first place. Our contribution, as consumers, must be not to demand the products made by wasting resources and subsidized by polluting air. This is hardheaded realism. The person who claims that conventional economics and conventional wisdom will serve us is really the impractical idealist.

What we ask is that ideals be ecologically realistic. Only ecological diversity and stability guarantee continued equal rights to anyone. Let us have an ecological perspective when we talk about equal rights for all people. It is always more important to *have* rights than to assure an evenhanded dividing up of them. It is going to be difficult to keep human diversity while assuring basic rights to all people. We might begin by realizing that making everyone like us is not assuring them equal rights! Ideals of affluence for ever-increasing numbers of people seem ecologically unrealistic. Perhaps we are wrong about this but, plainly, ignoring inevitable processes in nature will only result in disaster for everybody.

It may be a little unfair for critics of the Establishment such as leftists to say that we have put certain projects in the wrong perspective. What are they offering instead? We agree that the gargantuan South Mall project in Albany does not deserve top priority. That monumental transformation of a downtown capitol city into a governmental and cultural showpiece emphasizes buildings rather than nature or men. But what is *the* emphasis of social activism in society today? What is it in the ghettos? Maybe not on futuristic buildings but certainly on man-made objects. Not on nature. Not on ecology.

Maybe it is unfair to complain that some people buy plastic flowers while the roof leaks. Plastic gewgaws of all kinds are symptoms of a misguiding ideal. Homes are another. In renting or building the latter, we tend to buy beyond our means. There is, as with other, broader aspects of environment, a failure to estimate the amount of commitment to maintenance that should be part of the bargain parcel. A house, a technological economy, or a plastic tree in Disneyland does not, like a rose or an ecosystem, take care of itself. There is, thus, a great deal wrong with a plastic tree! A real tree not only grows itself, at no energetic or material expense to us; it performs useful functions for its ecosystem and the ecosystem's occupants.

When you consider also our destructive missionary efforts (as in Hawaii), destruction of American Indians, the record in Vietnam, the supersonic transport program, farm subsidies, and all nationalistic and egotistic aspects of the space program, it becomes clear that American society solidly promotes some dubious ideals. The mere presumption that "people come first," when people want impossible things, when society has misguided them, may not do much to rescue us from folly.

Legal and scientific ideals get us into trouble too. The notion that the individual is innocent until proved guilty is good for justice within a society. But it is neglect of sanity to allow it to act as an umbrella for corporate "individuals," so that we are exposed, because it profits somebody, to thermal pollution, pesticides, defoliation, irrigation, high-altitude air pollution, radiation injury, traffic jams, and slums.

Silence is very commonly misused in our society to prevent conservation and to enhance exploitation. A corporation is allowed to continue to use science in pursuit of its ecological misconduct while a legally hamstrung minority of society must prove—scientifically—that the corporation is guilty. Laws also give an individual the right to sell any wild plant growing on his land. Whether orchid or arbutus, the flower has no legal rights in most states. At its very roots, society fails to impress upon us that freedom does not mean license, but rather the privilege of interacting with the world around us. Freedom is, thus, a fragile planetary quality. At any one time, more people means less freedom per person, now and in the future. Misuse means degradation of the planet and, again, less freedom per person.

All this has relevance to the challenge of repair. Repair must be one of the goals of education. What is necessary is not the absolutism of a human dictator but the dictates of an aristocracy of responsibility and dedication. Great things must come from everyone. Neither a hereditary aristocracy nor a mindless, regimented bureaucracy will serve. Surprisingly enough, perhaps, it has rarely been better said than by Karl Marx. "Man," Marx wrote in an essay on Feuerbach and Hegel, "can make nothing without *nature,* without the *sensuous external* world. . . . Nature is the *inorganic body* of man. . . . Man *lives* by nature. This means that nature is his *body* with which he must remain in perpetual process in order not to die."

Where do we start? It is easy to oversimplify the problem. Curbing our population growth *is* important. To say that alone, however, is oversimplification, given that the numbers already on hand, with their wildly growing energy requirements, are sufficient to do us in. Nor is solving the energy-use problem enough. Energy is but motive force for the distribution of influence. And our influence comes in increasingly destructive and varied forms; snowmobiles, hovercraft, 500,000-ton oil tankers; cyclamates, DDT; strip mining, mining at the bottom of the sea; elegantly mechanized agriculture and forestry—you name it.

And where do these influences arise? In the minds of men, of course. Herein lies the grand dilemma. We are a society dedicated to the creative, the novel, the inventive. The development of the light bulb or of the Hula-Hoop means impact upon millions of people and the founding of industrial empires. At the same time, we decry the decline of places where people may play with Hula-Hoops. We deplore the loss of places where we may walk in darkness away from intruding street lamps.

How are we to proceed? Answers must operate along an extended front, in every direction and at the same time. It is unfair nonsense to assign the responsibilities and hopes for tomorrow to our children. What right have we to make whoopee and send them the bill? We are, so far, doing exactly that. It is unfair to expect manufacturers to stand the gaff while the consumer continues his demand for the kinds of products that have been deplored in this book.

A possible beginning? Make schools vital learning centers for all ages. Make schools vantage points from which to see everywhere. The genesis of that possible beginning is the subject of the final chapters of our book.

Part Five

Curing Miseducation

The self-confidence of learned people is the comic tragedy of civilization.

Alfred North Whitehead
Science and Philosophy

To promote perception is the only truly creative part of recreational engineering.

Aldo Leopold
A Sand County Almanac

The ecologist knows that the most interesting, beautiful and efficiently integrated type of habitat is that in which there is great variety. Superficially it might seem that industrialisation provides plenty of variety but it results in more and more people thinking in much the same way and with similar materialistic aspirations.

Edward A. Armstrong
The Folklore of Birds

Chapter 22

Proposing an Ecological Model

Ecology deals with wholeness. It is a science that leads from the classroom to ecosystems of great complexity, integrity, and fragility. Ecology introduces us to some of the most complex aspects of reality. It also illuminates the supremacy of processes over static parts of nature. Atoms, molecules, and individuals do exist, but too much concentration upon them is a dangerous distraction from the whole.

As urbane beings, we need to learn to ask questions that will yield not just a taking apart, but also a putting together. Such behavior befits a civilized organism whose behavior is productive of so many ecological events. What such a point of view will do to traditional ways of knowing, finding out, proving, and teaching is almost anybody's guess.

What kind of person will emerge from intense exposure to ecology? At the least, it will be one whose knowledge will be used in order to wonder, not to dispel wonder.

Who will teach? Exposure of students to a generous sample of nature is certainly going to be messy for overcrowded classes, overworked teachers, and harried, single-visioned curriculum administrators. But such an exposure is necessary. It is honest. It will sharpen curiosity, and challenge the best minds of the community. It is better than the contrivances of old-fashioned Disciplines and Departments. Even if mistakes are made, it is certainly more useful than hastening student alienation until it becomes a way of life.

Maybe we do live in a world of instant messages in an electronic universe. It is, however, a universe only in the sense that it is the only one most of us know. It is a pretty insignificant part of what can be felt, tasted, smelled, and heard here in a world of plants, animals, and seasons not yet quite flattened by our ideals or quantified by our computers.

We fall prey to our own verbal traps. Many nonbiological experts (some of them in biology departments) these days construct schemes and machines of great complexity of design. They use the resemblances of organisms to machines to prove that organisms are machines. This is not dangerous only because, as some people would have us believe, it is dangerous to humane values. It is very poor science to begin with. The approach tells us next to nothing about the impressive ways that organisms are not like machines.

Admittedly, the prospects of an age of ecological enlightenment are not overwhelmingly good. One of the reasons is that classical urban science has never been concerned with anything so elemental as Earth's *survival.* Earth, being providentially provided if not entirely theologically irrelevant, has been in practice taken for granted or even demeaned by most scientists. Scientists have pretty generally agreed with the theological and philosophical kingpins of our culture that values are not derived from land or nonhuman life. *Concern* has always been presumably taught by some other department of the school or university —and has always been a bit suspect anyway. However, it has to be emphasized that scientists have little precedent to guide them in building a responsible science. What discipline now tells us authoritatively that it is not enough to preserve Earth merely that our exploitation may become more efficient? Neither theology nor philosophy tells us unequivocally what to do with our science. The usual interpretation of their teaching is to increase our Gross National Product.

Our personal belief is that science is the domain of the individual, that it is the very personal matter of fitting oneself into the reality of this world. Science, in this sense, is nearly dead in our land. The first wounds resulted when vast sums of money were appropriated to support research in academic institutions. A scientist is now not up to snuff unless he has received the accolade of a grant from the National Science Foundation or the Ford Foundation. The values formed during the period of flush funding are with us still, although some of them look a little ill-made in less affluent lights.

The process of de-individualizing science, however, is still on the move. The President's message on science and technology delivered before Congress in March 1972 committed us to a corporate view of science and research. Understanding for the individual in a complicated world is replaced by a group dedication to troubleshooting in a game of eternal progress and growth. "I am therefore calling today for a strong new effort to marshall science and technology in the work of strengthening our economy and improving the quality of our life. And I am outlining ways in which the federal government can work as a more effective partner in this great task. . . . For one thing we have come to recognize that such innovation is essential to improving our economic productivity—to producing more and better goods and services at lower costs. . . . In the first place, we must always be aware that the mere act of scientific discovery alone is not enough. Even the most important breakthrough will have little impact on our lives unless it is put to use—and putting an idea to use is a far more complex process than has often been appreciated."

The President next accented the future role of federal agencies: the Atomic Energy Commission, National Aeronautics and Space Administration, National Bureau of Standards, National Institutes of Health, Fort Detrick, and National Center for Toxicological Research at Pine Bluffs, all of them agencies where, even at best, breadths of view will narrow and vulnerabilities will increase. (Vulnerability associated with centralization and specialization is surely no small matter. Diminished fuel supplies of the past years have accentuated our failures in the "architecting" of large buildings as well as large agencies.)

We overlook more recent developments of the role of science in government—or is it the other way round?—and only comment that it appears to us that the politicizing of science is a degrading affair. Exactly the same thing, of course, can be said for letting science serve some but not all individuals of a country.

Science has, unfortunately, been caught up in the common belief that a major part of its public use is to make exploitation of Earth more efficient. With that belief enshrined in our technological decalogue, we have grown fat on the proposition (which is but an extension) that it is better to extract now and let future generations pay the price. The responsible alternative—surely a sound subject for scientific exploration—is to internalize costs, distribute them equitably, and wait to grow naturally. We still hear only part of the story. It is very shortsighted of young people today to agree with certain of their hard-hatted elders that college kids are overeducated. Miseducated, perhaps. Unfortunately, the differences may not be clear to the public, including students.

One popular image of science is of an impersonal discipline, concerned only with exactitude, prediction, and duplicability. Another view is of science as problem-oriented technology in a society that has already made up its mind about the meaning of ecological responsibility. Our search is for a science that is better than either of these views. We wish for more education and better education, education that keeps all portals of the intellect open.

Miseducation has kept us from a rich experience. We spend our lives in classrooms from which nature is excluded. In losing contact with the natural world, we fail to understand our place in it. In our naivete, we commit many blunders. The bombing of Stanford University's linear accelerator center on December 7, 1971 is one example.

There is plenty of so-called education, of course. We live in "an economy of misdirected abundance," as Lewis Mumford has reminded us. Education still fails to touch many people. In some of those it does touch, there emerges a tense feeling of helplessness that dampens effective action. This does not mean that super-optimistic Pollyannas ought to emerge from classrooms. But it does mean that some current inaction shows as much lack of commitment based on lack of knowledge about alternatives as it does conviction of hopelessness.

Miseducation harms people in other ways. It distorts moralities. People can no longer respond to Emerson's directive to save on the lower levels and spend on the higher. American spending behavior is, in fact, frequently quite the opposite. Our first, most pressing demands are for glass bottles that can be discarded, aluminum throwaway beer cans, paper plates, and lurid newspapers that we finally cannot get rid of fast enough even for our own safety. Then, of course, when an insulted environment kicks back, we dare not ask for higher things until the throwaways have been disposed of. Higher things have to wait! And . . . how do we order our hopes? Do we hope only that we can manage to clean up the mess? Do we settle for hoping that Earth will stop retching back into our laps the messes we have long thought out of sight? Under such circumstances, hope is not only an inflatable goddess but a pathogenic one.

Institutional education will not be complete until all aspects of human society and the remnants of nonhuman nature have made their contributions. Somehow, we have forgotten that the real classroom is the whole world and that we are all in it.

How can this be remedied? First, realize that estrangement is due to urbanized separation of human beings from primary environment. The answer is to bring environment back into the city, especially into its institutional schools. We have to learn (that is, *children have to be taught*) that real wealth of water, soil, air, and living things is different from symbolic wealth and that neither nature nor society can offer us resources gratis. Water does not come from a faucet. Water is not only a unique commodity but it can also teach us about the three great ecological fluxes: matter, energy, and information.

Estrangement can be overcome by encounter visits to crisis areas, landfill sites, sewer outfalls, junkyards, power plants, and endangered wild areas. Such visits must involve key people of both the visiting and the visited institutions. They ought to be featured in the press. Visits will prompt more visits. The world will become more real through the process of learning. Nor will the knowledge gained lose any of its immediacy if one heard offenders named in public, or if students had direct access to officials of accused companies and governmental institutions. With communication established, understanding and action might easily follow.

Education can heal estrangement if students are led to see that political and corporate boundaries can be spiteful and divisive. Lakes are units, wherever the property lines fall. The ocean rightfully belongs to everyone. Rivers belong to everyone, too, including the fish. Dumping and polluting ought to draw the same hurt response that would come if someone stuffed garbage into your coat pocket. Find out where detergents come from—and why. Look out for biocides. Search for evidence that our soil is being used as a dumping ground for environmental quack medicines.

Surely, with this approach, the education of parents will follow. Surely, they will have something of value to contribute to the education of the young. In the encounter of these two supposedly opposed groups, we might learn much about some really serious social questions. How, for example, are parents ensuring that their children will not live in a world where the right to drive a car is rationed? What are the parents of today doing to assure their children a chance to live on green land? What can they tell each other about family planning and birth control? About respect for others (smoking and transistorized radios)? About life goals? Adult education deserves to be more than what is legitimized by an evening class certificate.

The technique is clear. Learn how the social community works as well as how the ecological community functions. Starting with the latter, see how the former can be made a better guide to a full life. Think about controls not in terms of repression but of conservation of rights and of options that are now being lost because of environmental deterioration, overpopulation, and resource depletion. Consider the nature of the creative process. Think about the wisdom of evaluating inventions before they are released to fatten upon the environment to the profit of a few and the loss of everybody. Make projects into real teamwork. Convert confrontations with civic leaders into fruitful activity. Turn teacher training into real work .

Chapter 23

What Has Gone Wrong with Learning?

Some things are apparent about people in general in the urban world. Certain attitudes emerge as urban people work their world views into reality. Most of us have grown up on a view of man as a tender shoot that requires the umbrella of culture and high technology. Otherwise, we are told, we should wilt under the dire influences of a cruel environment. Who has not heard that life for man, before the blessings of Western civilization arrived at its perfection, was "nasty, brutish and short"? As a matter of fact, people are tougher than most ecologically dominant nonhuman, nonurban organisms. The major exceptions are those hardy plants called weeds and those devious organisms, all small, that manage to crack our defenses and make us sick.

This toughness is not entirely to our advantage. It means that as long as peregrine falcons die from pesticides before we do, we shall feel no compulsions to stop the manufacture and spread of chlorinated hydrocarbon pesticides. It means that if forests disappear from radiation injury before we do, we shall not much bother to curb radiation.

Unfortunately, there is no surefire answer. Science can too easily become only a technique to tell us what happened, after disaster has hit. That kind of science will not help us much.

The urbanite has not been taught to distinguish between one kind of forest and another or even between a real forest and one made of plastic. *Simplicity* is not the threat to him that it is to the ecologist who sees ecological simplicity as harbinger of ecosystemic doom. Simplicity may even, so far as urban reality is concerned, be desired. Central Park without its trees and shrubbery would harbor fewer potential robbers. But how do we mean to save ourselves? Most of us are preservationists at least up to that point! If we cannot save the whooping crane, how do we know that we can save ourselves?

The urbanite in the magnificent complexity of natural wilderness, although not in danger, tends to be uncomfortable. He may even think he is suffering from sensory deprivation. As a matter of fact, his eyes, ears, nose, and other sensory structures are receiving stimuli that are strange to him. Only a new education would allow him to weigh input and choose rationally which stimuli to respond to. Natural variety, under such circumstances, is too foreign and low-key to stimulate him, regardless of its role in enabling the ecosystem to sustain human life.

Land not transformed is, to the urbanite, wild and not subject to civilization's rules. This is probably one of the reasons for the destruction that is meted out to all natural things in the city. We comprehend the character of repair of built things but in our lack of contact with other organisms, fail to understand their vulnerability. It may also be related to the dislike people have of broad spaces of land in cities, especially public land where the usual urban roles do not prevail. Is it unrealistic to hope for land enough to give to people to deform as they wish, to remodel in their own images, just to see if it will work? Maybe rooftop gardens, tanks of soil on porch ledges, or window gardens offer some promise. But how much do people need? And what degree of private ownership is necessary before respect can arise? Can people be reeducated to love commonly owned land? As long as we continue to deprive people of contact with nature on the one hand, and assault them with dramatic but sterile architected wonderlands on the other, we are not going to find out.

It is not simply that wild land is too wild for the urbanite. Its variety is just not seen. Natural landscapes, even pastoral ones, are seen as featureless. We urbanites feel compelled to shape lawns, mold shrubbery, align trees. The aim is a maximum of some sort of visual stimulation (and even that is so one-sided that a deformed hedge takes precedence over a varied landscape whose parts we refuse to learn about). Vision is a tyrant over the other senses. It is also an ecological robber. Yosemite is so crowded that visitors—most of whom go there merely to look—might as well be in a trailer park. The environment there is actually deteriorating physically. Niagara is not great enough as a falls. Even harnessing its power with generators is not enough. It has to be decorated with colored lights.

All right: so what? These facts gain greater relevance to the urbanite when the same attitude that crowds Yosemite hammers the costly stones for the wedding-cake baroque of the New York State capitol building. The tyranny of the contrived visual causes billions to be spent on urban renewal projects that are deserted much of the twenty-four-hour period. We cannot let the same monocular view of the simplicity of the rose garden loose in a beech-maple forest—that is, if we wish the forest to remain stable and fertile.

Because urban man lives a centralized existence, he applies his ideal everywhere. Thus, schools, waste-treatment plants, food sources, and information-control centers are all piled up on one another. That this is not the ideal ecological solution is seen when we note that we are also centralizing wastes into our groundwater, pollutants into our air, and concrete over productive soils. That it may not be an ideal social solution either may soon become clearer. We now have one chemist and a dozen or less assistants who are responsible for the treatment of water supplies for many thousands of townspeople. We typically concentrate the responsibility for sewage treatment (a "lower-class" activity!) upon the shoulders of even fewer men.

The linearity and angularity of the urban world are extended to all nature. In matters of residential hedges, it may well be everyone to his own taste. A road, a power-line right-of-way, or a furrow up a hillside, however, are insults that we have to pay for many times over.

Domination of man in the city can be expected, although we do suggest that it has been overdone. The domination of man in nature outside of the city is quite another matter. Why are people so unyielding? That the urban approach has not worked very well is obvious. What is readily apparent is that life just does not have to be lived that way.

The city is structurally fairly simple (for all the confusion of the unrecycled remains that clutter its avenues). We are now carrying its message of simplicity everywhere. Similarly, complexity and challenge in the city are conquered by simplification. An asphalt parking lot is simpler to maintain if it is vast and open, uninterrupted by trees or other diversifying objects. Schools are less of a custodial problem if the halls are straight and provide easy movement of equipment. Trees, shrubs, streams, and ponds are a nuisance around the school because they are awkward to maintain and because they become unsightly under the influence of so many children. Dark, shadowy wooded areas are dangerous and may serve to conceal illicit activities. So the growth of the modern city is guided by the desire to exclude the complex and the uncontrollable. Yet our cities become more uncontrollable every day, as they will continue to do unless we restore them to a living balance where living things control themselves. Living things, under any other circumstance, tend to become uncontrollable as long as they are alive; but even the physical aspects of Earth look less easily controllable than they did a few years ago. Our simplification out there has not worked either.

The one thing that the urban system has not simplified is quantity and quality of information. Nor could it and live. It is time that we urbanites realized that the destruction of nonhuman information through destruction of nature will not allow us to live either. We suggest that Ivan Illich has it right—and that repair might begin right in the heart of urbanism:

> Life today in New York produces a very peculiar vision of what is and what can be, and without this vision life in New York is impossible. A child on the streets of New York never touches anything which has not been scientifically developed, engineered, planned, and sold to someone. Even the trees are there because the Parks Department decided to put them there. The jokes the child hears on television have been programmed at a high cost. The refuse with which he plays in the streets of Harlem is made of broken packages planned for somebody else. Even desires and fears are institutionally shaped. Power and violence are organized and managed: the gangs versus the police. Learning itself is defined as the consumption of subject matter, which is the result of researched, planned, and promoted programs. Whatever good there is, is the product of some specialized institution. It would be foolish to demand something which some institution cannot produce. The child of the city cannot expect anything which lies outside the possible development of institutional process. Even his fantasy is prompted to produce science fiction. He can experience the poetic surprise of the unplanned only through his encounter with "dirt," blunder, or failure: the orange peel in the gutter, the puddle in the street, the breakdown of order, program, or machine are the only take-offs for creative fancy. "Goofing off" becomes the only poetry at hand.[1]

What we want to do is to increase choices, not minimize them. How do you keep choices? Shall we let uninformed taste make the ultimate decisions? Certain zoning regulations amount to that. But shall we suppose that choices are so trivial that we can simply let ourselves be underbid?

What constitutes a *safe* answer to the ecosystemic breakdown we face? Certainly we should scrap all plans to relieve congestion, smog, and sewage by spreading them out over the surface of Earth. Certainly we should plan for far more intangible, far more precious, activities. Prudence suggests that we ought to plan for a more varied and higher-quality diet for a smaller total world population. To adapt to high-quality fuel resources such as solar power. To plan for a world climate not endangered by Earth's most ingenious inhabitant. To protect a

[1]Ivan Illich, *Deschooling Society,* Harper, New York, 1970, p. 108.

host of animal and plant species from extinction by guaranteeing them plenty of their natural habitat. An even distribution of human numbers may do nothing but guarantee that one day all problems will be worldwide and equally insoluble everywhere.

All of this is closely tied to the quality of choices we make. We could choose to steal all the water from Canada and Alaska, over their citizens' dead bodies, if necessary. We could, with it, then build overflow cities galore on the deserts of Nevada and Utah. But ought we to do so? Shall we continue to subsidize the paving of prime farmland for new cities and suburbs? Are we going to talk about the freedom to have children, when sheer numbers alone cut into the qualities of all freedoms, including the freedoms of those children? Can we stand the restrictions brought by numbers? Will we tolerate the necessary regulations that are needed to keep dense settlements alive? Can we adjust to the boredom of loss of contact with natural reality? Actually, we are already making these decisions—in ways that make it seem that we believe a divine providence will save us from error.

Finally, can we control the quality of our cities? Not the mere shell of the city but the quality of people who live in them? We are still building cities, and old ones are growing less controllable every minute. Maybe we had better admit that we do not know everything about city building, and let that precaution slow our activities. We might heed the parable of Thurber's moth, who claimed that *he* had invented the flame—that it would do his bidding. Had we better not include in our equations for building cities the probability that some people will remain just as belligerent, as unfeeling, and as neurotic as some of them have been throughout historic time? Man's belligerency is a product of nature, and thus nature in adequate quantities may be the best antidote. The man-made city provides few targets for violence other than man and his products and the few natural targets available are overwhelmed. The solutions thus become the proper balancing of the equation of men and other living things.

Is making everyone equally affluent the answer? Can it be done? Hospital costs per day, for example, went up from $5.21 in 1946 to $32.54 in 1967 to $45.01 in 1969. (1973: Even a *ward room* in our local hospital costs $51.94 per day.) Show us poor people (who need hospital care most) who can realistically hope to keep ahead of that kind of affluence! It is probable that we need something that is new, something better than the provision of cities for the benefit of the affluent class, whether that class is old, new, or future.

Since the city molds men even while man is making the city, it follows that we need better cities. Western urban man swapped the mysterious orderliness of the universe for a designed world, and the city is to some extent the supreme product of his design. Doctrine, material wealth and power have become more important than personal experience or the awe felt in actually being alive in the created world of all nature. In a society dominated by the urban life style, the design of the city has been applied to the whole world. At least one good reason for refusing to support that domination any longer is that it has not worked very well.

Chapter 24

Education for Real

We can diversify the sterile urban environment ecologically. Maybe we can also diversify it socially. The key to social diversity is to find ways of encouraging the individual to comprehend his participation in a self-sustaining environment. Focus first upon restoring holistic, ecosystemic environments. Peoples' education of themselves will follow naturally. The spoon-feeding of traditional institutional education perpetuates only spoon-fed knowledge. In the process, responsibilities shift to others. We have become the more vulnerable for it. Man's tutor for a million years was the primal environment, and confrontations that are undertaken with directness and resolution can still teach us well.

We suggest neither that problems be tackled in a thoughtlessly abrupt way nor that present social conditions continue indefinitely. But let us start.

We need educational thinking that binds us to a broader approach than traditional educational disciplines have done. The latter, in their efforts to keep off each others' toes, have actually built into themselves an unwillingness and inaptitude for dealing with real problems. Real social situations (shot through with genius, with the unique contributions of individuals) are not academically bounded and patterned. To the academician, they seem a hodgepodge, even though they are always profoundly coherent and finely woven—in ways that escape his attention. Thus, we know curiously little about how to cure social ills or how to participate in a natural existence.

The grafting on of schools and classes in environmental science *is not* what we need. There are too many divisive structures and narrowing barriers in educational centers now. We do need a refocusing of intellect upon man-environment interactions that involve direct physical experience. This can, unhappily, occur in few existing classrooms and can be taught in few of the carefully overprogrammed days of teachers who now must try to make living sense of administrative nonsense. We fool only ourselves if we confuse a true reordering with programs designed to correct such short-term errors as are involved in pollution control. It is possible to turn caring for the good Earth into something more satisfying than that.

The biosphere is fragile and finite; yet it is vibrant with promises of survival that are lacking in the city. It is a whole, within which the determining factors are diverse and self-sustaining forms and processes. Our diverse responsibility for that whole is one of the keys to its survival. Man shapes more than his own future when he shapes the environment. Knowing that, we can if we wish come to think creatively about forming without deforming. Thinking about the future is a condition of survival. And one of the conditions of survival is thinking of man as only part of the future.

Call it Art or call it Science. Maybe what it is depends upon little more than the emphasis given to its refined parts. In any case, the answer falls within the domain of planned enrichment of experience for human beings. Another name for it is education. Education is devoted to the common social goal of providing each human being with an enlightening wealth of daily experiences and responsibilities. Such exposure will allow him to realize his potential within the framework of a social system and a life style that are realistic parts of the ecosystem. The aim is a familiarity with the many parts of the bioshpere that breeds respect and not contempt.

Everyone knows that education is costly. In 1963, the price tag for educating the children of about 190 million Americans was more than that spent for all governmental functions in India, a nation of 460 million people. Not only is the cost high, it is directly related to high population densities and to a downward shift in age distribution so that there are more young people of school age per tax-producing adult. Most money crises in education are intimately related to the people explosion.

High postwar growth of young people has created a crushing tax rate. That has been followed by taxpayer complaints, governmental economy drives, and dismay over the quality of education. Taxpayers, remember, pay not just for education, whether they have children or not. They also pay for increasing medical costs, relief programs, governmental expenses, international aid, space races, and wars.

What can be done about the real problem of high growth rates causing declining quality of education?

First, buy less costly "hardware" and do not confuse an education with mere attendance at a school. Invest in a piece of good wild land that requires little more than that it be left alone. It can educate and instruct endlessly any number of well-behaved people. There can be few charges that the land is being wasted. Even if it fails to educate a passerby today, his time may come tomorrow or the next day. A patch of beech trees and violets costs nothing for upkeep. A well-placed path costs little to maintain and it is there as long as it is needed and used.

Contrast the low cost, cheap maintenance, and perpetual usefulness of a school forest with the money wasted on an apartment swimming pool that a few people use only a few days of the year. Consider the expense of an electron microscope that sits idle much of the time. And how justified is it to add the high costs of building construction to "the high cost of education?" Buildings are necessary, of course; but they might be constructed to reveal natural environment rather than obliterate it. The elaborate elegance of many school buildings adds little to quality of education but it virtually guarantees an affluent income to unionized labor and professional architects. Although this kind of building may give the construction community a vested interest in what is called education, it does little to lessen popular criticism of high professorial salaries or to soften the harsh views that nearby landowners have of students.

Second, education can be given a societywide base. A firm and sensitive commitment to education should lead to use of all the commonly present media of information dispersal. The media need but be turned to productive uses. There is room for increased, integrated attention to environmental matters all along the line. Out in the world of nature, we can protect firmly what is left. We can replace wisely where that is possible. That results in education *for* something. We can introduce into the restored environments sensitive indicator species; when those species die, we shall know that something is wrong.

Third, we can deformalize formal education. In that whole field today, preschool through high school and college, we question whether what we are doing is what needs to be done. Not only is there room for changes in course patterns; some of what we do needs to be stopped. There is room for ecologically oriented programs that could produce within a generation the best-educated people we have ever known. But it cannot be done if we make only the technical professions our aim in education (and in our lives). It cannot be done if we make each school grade merely a little version of the one ahead, for some of the things we do in the advanced grades fall singularly short of environmental wholeness.

Students are a little embarrassed to love and feel things when they become high school or college residents. It would be good if primary grade students walked along forest paths and waded in ponds instead of having their heads stuffed with literary images unrelated to what they see in the real world. From such primary foundations, all roads could lead outward, providing real and varied options. Education should consist of being exposed to and taking some of those options. Only within such a complex and diversified experience can people assess their own inclinations, capabilities, and aptitudes. This requires guidance by talented and responsible people. It also requires the rocks, sticks, bugs, and flowers that ought to have precedence over book learning.

How do schools measure up to these (or even their own stated) aims today? Not very well, we believe. Judging from what is said and from what is available as a measuring stick, schools are architecturally and environmentally sterile. They are dominated by hurricane fences, parking lots, and tenderly nursed and featureless lawns. Their structure is insipid, cavernous, and regimented. They are only now and then really creature-comfortable. Their designs maximize economy, surveillance, safety and—maybe—efficiency. It may be unfair to call them places of detention but they certainly inspire little pride or allegiance.

School sites are abandoned for the three most ecologically vibrant months of the year; our notions of leisure effectively sterilize the three months that we are free. Schools are usually empty by four o'clock every day and on weekends. Notwithstanding the remarkable dedication of many teachers, most of them go to the school only because they are paid to do so. It is unlawful for students to go elsewhere. Adults see the inside of their school buildings only if sufficiently riled by new taxes or sex education, or because their night school course requires attendance.

And we continue to build more such institutions—many more. Some of these are not just costly—but very costly. A good example is the justly celebrated campus of the State University of New York at Albany. Leaving aside the $100 million price tag (since grown larger), the ecological illogic is enough to make either educator or taxpayer wince. Part of the mistake was taking formerly beautiful urban recreational land of diverse quality and making it into a homogenized event. Part was the scraping and leveling of distinctively modeled topography. Part was the complete obliteration of richly varied forest clumps and the extravagantly costly planting of a very few exotic species of trees and shrubs in rows, ranks, and phalanxes. And part is the cost of maintenance of lawns that have to be watered and mowed and soils that have to be planted, herbicided, fertilized, pesticided—

not only today but tomorrow and tomorrow and tomorrow. The mistake has been abuse of potential, a failure of understanding and a botch of efficient participation.

The consequences? We extract, isolate, and estrange our most sensitive people, at a stage of their existence when they are most in search of a guiding pattern. It is not just that they are cut off from society for twenty or more of their formative years. They are cut off from learning from and responding to nature at a time when the most pleasing and lasting impressions are made.

Add to this deprivation during youth the disenfranchisement of those over sixty-five. In man's first cultures, the old were the wise, the bearers of good guidance. Now, we must assume, the voices of wisdom lie elsewhere. The presumably adult operators of information-storage and -retrieval systems thus live a brief existence, sandwiched between their isolated youth and unused old age. Is real citizenship for all ages out of the question?

Why do you avoid going to school whenever possible? What would you like to do there? Are there schools that accomplish what you think worth doing? Forget for a minute financial limitations. What ought schools to do for you? Are there any concrete, common social goals any more? What about equipping individuals to perform well in society, in an experience-rich life style that conforms to principles of nature? Here, nature includes human nature and the social structures of man and wild nature.

As a beginning, this means bringing students into closer contact with functioning society. Television could, in this way, be made to work for society. It means visits to branches of government. It means taking branches of government into schools—not just administrative funnymen, but, for example, the city planner's office and laboratory. What an enrichment of social experience for students that would be to see and understand the planner's local and regional maps, his daily work, his armory of statistics!

Schools can be sited at vantage points—by lakeside, riverfront, hilltop. "It would be," said Thoreau, "no small advantage if every college were thus located at the base of a mountain. It is as good at least as one well-endowed professorship." The community could be seen, the effects of community actions could be monitored.

Meteorological and health department samplings and recorders can be placed within school grounds and buildings. Foul air, dirty water, diseased trees can then become known and alleviative efforts can be followed stage by stage (and enforced by popular support). As a part of every school experience, air-filter data, particle counts, temperature and humidity statistics can be gathered and understood by every student. Furthermore, births, deaths, and reasons for dying should be as evident as the clock on the wall.

Structural and engineering approaches can be thought of. Leave forests intact. Encourage forests if they are not already there. Let joe-pye weed bloom on campus. Fully protected forests can abut buildings and windows can look out onto them. Wings of buildings can elbow into forests. Students can then see, hear, and smell forests without destroying them by thoughtless foot pressure. Forest can even be brought inside buildings at focal points. Let iris gardens and vegetable patches, cared for by students, replace grass.

We find it hard to be patient with plaints that children will not respect one anothers' plantings, that they will not be able to care for their gardens or animals, that they will lose interest in the course of the growing season, that the school year is not compatible with cycles of planting and harvesting. Surely, these criticisms suggest their own cures.

Poetry, biology, chemistry, history: every course taught in schools could, with searching, find its roots firmly planted in the soil. Parents might also find themselves returning to the soil, just as many parents today are learning the joy of cooking from their rebelling children who have learned that our cuisine is as dull as the life it feeds.

The need for rapport between plant and planter, animal and husbandman, speaks loudly enough. Most educators, however, pointedly ignore that need. They mistakenly push it aside not only as merely vocational training but as training that is not suitable for urban dwellers. They blink at the fact that only a thorough education in the ways of the real world can provide us with a society resilient enough to adapt to (or avoid) revolution. They forget that mainland China now successfully educates its citizens to love the land and know its ways intimately. Whether we agree with them or not, their knowledge of the biosphere, at very least, puts them at a competitive advantage over the ill-informed products of our educational system. In vital long-term ways, our educators have chosen to overlook the fact that our educations are mere vestiges, shorn of the meanings they once had, and that rigidity, however highly enthroned, limits innovation.

Our lives lack even the culturally precious symbols of nature (rock, water, vegetation) that characterize Japanese gardens. Our lives now lack the positive learning that comes from a natural failure, whether caused by drought, storm, or insects. Even the very young can learn the splendors of patience, as has been well written by economist Nicholas Georgescu-Roegen:

> We cannot mine the stock of solar energy at a rate to suit our desires of the moment. We can use only that part of the sun's energy that reaches the globe at the rate determined by its position in the solar system. With the stocks of low entropy in the earth's crust we may be impatient and, as a result, we may be impatient—as indeed we are—with their transformation into commodities that satisfy some of the most extravagant human wants. But not so with the stock of sun's energy. Agriculture teaches, nay, obliges man to be patient—a reason why peasants have a philosophical attitude in life pronouncedly different from that of industrial communities.[1]

Neighboring homes can be located with pride with reference to a really functioning schoolyard of responsible students. Local architects and planners can then think of ways to guide builders, garden clubs, and preservation societies in getting the most life out of the forest and the most life into human society. With ecologically alert interactions at the community level, any sickness of the environment will act as a red light for concerned remedial action. Community rescue will not be the self-interested covering up of pollution or the culverting underground of a dirty stream.

Think about preserving diversity in total community efforts. Diversify not just recreation, play, and plantings. Vary the

[1]Nicholas Georgescu-Roegen, *The Entropy Law and the Economic Process,* Harvard, Cambridge, Mass., 1971, p. 297.

landscape productively with agriculture, horticulture, dairying, and poultry production. This cannot happen, of course, if feeding ourselves is a shameful activity; nor can it happen if the urban market drives land prices upward and town taxes skyrocket in the so-called free economy. (It is questionable that an economy that denies one the opportunity to preserve his ecosystem is a very free one.) Exposure to the many facets of an ecologically and economically relevant social life is absent from childrens' lives today. Such varied experiences lead to understanding of economic problems and an appreciation for ecological solutions that the study of economics alone will never do. The ultimate point of this is the poorest dwelling need not lack an ecological setting. There need be no lack of pride of ownership in any life-supporting contributor to the entire ecosystem. Nor need anyone lack an understanding of his own impact upon the ecosystem.

Why not cheaper education? There is no reason why saving money ought not be a virtue at civic as well as individual levels. Consider the value of having community individuals perform duties of real responsibility in school, both in maintenance and planning. In addition to patrons from the community, there can be student responsibilities, too. Windows can be cleaned, floors polished. This need not be so much forced labor as a chance for the exercise of responsibility.

Cheaper education? Some kinds of relatively inexpensive machine-assisted instruction may turn out to be more "personal" than the frantic kind of attention that large groups of students get in classrooms now. It might be questioned, too, whether the structured, nine-to-three day is best for everybody. We could phase vacations so that not everybody is at Yosemite at the same time. Freeing some professorial time by machine instruction might liberate both teacher and student for more valuable apprentice contacts.

Our aim is not to make education a better baby-sitter. Education's job is to undertake what cannot be done better by other agencies of the human mind and society. What that overall effort might try to achieve is what this book has been largely about. We have no illusions that American colleges and universities are places to start much of the true education that we envision. Such places lack holistic community feelings and functional local ties. We tend to wager our hopes on younger people in preschools, elementary schools, and high schools. The kind of learning we envision will count for more there. However, massive bureaucratizations of uniform school systems, even here, leave us only modest hopes—hopes that, somehow, small and local miracles will occur and that the news of their success will be heard round the world.

Chapter 25

The Environmental Ombudsman

The last point on education to be made takes us back into the community in all its complexity. It puts to work what we know and it welds man and nature into the natural unit that many people instinctively search for. It is a new urbanism that is truly urbane and has ecological heart to it.

Education does not stop in school nor must its effects end there. As educated citizens in the community, we can stop population growth. We can prevent profits on the speculation in land. We can apply against those who pollute the remedial social pressures that are cheaper and far more effective than legal action and fines, especially against individuals.

We can do more. We can discourage wrong actions when regulations are applied. There was, for example, a run on the market for DDT when it was reported to have been outlawed. There was a similar spending spree for cyclamates when they were banned as artificial sweeteners.

We can recognize the need for new information. We can ensure that priorities in research are geared to the needs of the community as well as the needs of industry. A host of problems that every gardener and homeowner wrestles with remain unsolved.

We can also support legislation aimed at conserving natural resources and natural beauty in this country. We can support agencies and groups that foster such conservation. We can elect politicians who will write and pass laws that assess the environmental impact of processes and devices before they become part of someone's vested interest.

It is time we started refusing to settle for a definition of ecological rescue as the art of the highly improbable. But to do that, we have to integrate ecological concern and informed prudence into community life at every level.

Here we face another dilemma. Federal and state governments are not notably good places to begin conserving environments. As action agencies, they have varied shortcomings. Most people think that political power sufficient for real action on a problem must issue from the highest governmental levels. The source of this illusion is that, as things now operate, local laws restricting a polluting industry that employs local people are soon made useless, if ever enacted, by the industry's threat to move to the next town. States face the same problem when businessmen suggest the possibility of moving into a more cooperative state. The ultimate appeal is to the federal government. The federal government, however, is subject to influence and even control by lobbyists. Such shrill minorities as the oil and automobile companies spend millions to twist the democratic route of representation to favor their interests. To top it off, federal decisions are riddled by ignorance of local conditions, weak in innovative maneuverability, and vulnerable to breakdown.

The hope of governing ourselves ecologically thus returns, beaten but wiser, from Washington to the classroom. The question is whether the job can be done and whether it can be done without spending more than the many billions of dollars already ill-spent on bureaucratic management and mismanagement of resources. If it is to be done without adding to the burden of bureaucratic myopia in policy guidance, we ourselves must do the job.

All this sharpens the need for a better-educated citizenry. It does not mean that we simply abdicate to local industry or to local government, which is local industry's frequent helpmeet. What is good for the local meat-packer may not be good for the whole community.

Knowing that community activities have produced plenty of examples where environmental damages were done, sometimes unwittingly, sometimes avoidably, F. Raymond Fosberg once proposed that there be a community ecologist in every city. The need is clear for independent judgment, legally empowered, to tone down the empire builders and the vociferous promoters at industrial, community, and governmental levels. Even granting that all conventional leaders are honest, their need for reliable and timely ecosystemic information—*before they commit themselves*—has never been more critical.

It seems that an *environmental ombudsman* is what is needed. In New Zealand, the ombudsman is empowered to receive and report grievances against the government. Power is needed. It has to be real power that is informed, expert, alertly concerned, wise in the ways of the region: and it has to be power commensurate with other powers in the community and unfettered by those powers' often quite explicit mandates of exploitation. What is desired is some way that a community can secure the necessary information for justified action and the power to carry it out, the necessary resilience for stable perpetuation of itself, and the unique local flavor of action that matches real needs and capacities.

The ombudsman would have professional responsibility for environmental manipulation of the community. Before we are accused of planning to get the most out of the natural community as quickly as possible, let us hasten to say that we consider the health of the community at least as important as that of its individual citizens and just as deserving of M.D.-level supervision. The ombudsman should have the same sort of independence of local whims that the doctor ideally has. We also propose that he be as free from public pressures, as free from legal traps, as autonomously provided with information, as uncompromised in his prescriptions as the respected doctor is. The ombudsman *is not* to be considered the soul or conscience of society, for we consider those functions properly restricted to responsible individuals only.

Some of the ombudsman's functions may be outlined tentatively. He might limit, through prescription, all chemicals that are to be used in the open environment. He might license the cutting of all native trees. He might issue permits for planting introduced species of plants, whether by government or individuals. He might approve landscaping plans for areas exceeding one-eighth acre in size. (The precedent for the last is not any harder to find than the nearest zoning regulation; this normally enforces little more than snob practice but it could be turned into a vital tool for saving us from ourselves.) He should certainly review and comment upon environmentally oriented programs presented by both state and private schools at all levels. He would participate in all litigation related to environmental degradation, as, for example, suits of a private citizen against a factory suspected of air or water pollution. He would approve municipal planning and initiate plans for vest-pocket or other parks and downtown nature refuges. He would pass on transit routings and sites of highways, airports, and hovercraft terminals.

There is no doubt of the need for such a person in every community. Look at the shams that our cities and towns are, in their feeble pretense of including nature in their plans and in their real submission to power and growth. There is no doubt that university, state, and professional examiners could now provide competent examinations for a nonprofessional man, yet give him a rank commensurate with the professional rank of lawyers, doctors, and dentists. His expert and custom-tailored advice could be provided for and funded at the local level. All that is needed is income tax reductions to make it possible. That is to say, his funding would come from his clients, from all of us.

It is improbable that adequate help will ever filter down from above to accomplish what needs to be done. On the other hand, the costs that do filter down will be higher and higher. The emphasis upon local funding and local action will, therefore, pay for itself. It is equivalent to money spent on preserving personal health rather than on hospitals for treating the sick. In fact, in the very needful work of cleaning up pollution, the environmental ombudsman would pay for himself in his services to that field alone.

Make no mistake about it. These gossamer threads that we have laid out are fragile. They will nowhere firmly support us unless we act with uncommon decision and with exceptional faith. They arise from the teachings of nature, however, and they can lead us out of the maze. Our own conviction is that they may prove more enduring than the steel and concrete that we have so far depended upon.

Chapter 26

Epilogue: The Tyranny of Time

Time is not on our side.

Nor is time ours alone, as Americans. Perhaps we could, if we set about it, repair the stresses in our society, the injuries showing openly in our countryside. But our time is also the time of Latin America, Africa, and Asia, overcrowded and underfed. Their birthrates are up to $2^1/_2$ times our own. Their population growth rates are three times as great, their total population far larger, their dependency loads of young persons greater, their potential for further growth truly explosive. In contrast, their capacity to buy affluence is pitifully small.

Perhaps it is fair to ask if there is really an *our* and *their* side.

We spin our fine theories of changing society. Our whole social fabric is torn by change. But biological time has not changed. We still have our individual, inherited daily rhythms, locked into a twenty-four-hour pattern that is as old as our cells. Babies require a gestation period that has not changed in millennia. Although we speed up our rates of resource depletion and use, the rates of growth of plants and animals do not change much, even under genetic management. Forests still measure their generations in centuries. Ecosystems may require a thousand years to attain their majority. A city, may, if it wants to, easily repair an injury. Your own body, however, takes its own time in healing a wound, and repair of a watershed (*real* repair, not just elimination of the worst pollutants) or the engineering of a wilderness will take scores or hundreds of years. A human population that has been growing rapidly continues to grow for many years even if its birth rate falls to a replacement value for its reproductive members.

Our story, which you have just read, has been a pretty gloomy one. How can we say that we are right when so many prophets of the past have been proved wrong? For one thing, the human species is part of a one-way flow of events; the thermodynamic law of entropy cannot be repealed. We have found numerous ways of making rates of destruction overbalance rates of building. The latter rates are biological, chemical, and geological rates that we can do little to influence, even when we want consciously to build rather than to destroy.

We have dispersed into virtually unrecoverable tiny particles the resources that were formerly richly concentrated. The geographical frontiers are no more. A look at our little globe (our privilege, thanks to Gemini and Apollo flights) in the firmament of space's almost universal blank shows a tiny sphere. Upon its limited, lucent surface, any move you make ultimately brings you back to your starting place. That is the only exact return possible upon this Earth. You cannot return to the same time, the same resources. Extinction of a species of animal or plant occurs only once. Just as irrecoverable is use of fossil fuels.

People who believe those who say that "Science will save us" had better listen to better-informed prophets. The new prophets do not fear just for a particular society or religion, as have doom sayers of the past. (We might point out, however, that the Jeremiahs who predicted the downfall of Rome were right.) Their predictions are based on much more realistic and sophisticated scientific data. Their fears are for the ecological underpinnings of *any* society of men.

We have, in our book, tried to avoid too much partisanship in the controversies among various modern prophets. Our general feelings about their theories will be obvious, although we trust that it will not be thought that we consider them equally well informed. It is not healthy to be too innocent in this world, and readers need to know that there are scientists moved more by the narrow precepts of ecologically ill-taught religious doctrines and by dreams of technological power than by science. Thus, Colin Clark, a British economist converted to Catholicism, proves to his satisfaction that human populations can grow to 47 billions and still be well-fed (and to 157 billion and survive). Such zealousness perhaps overlooks a simple but profound Christian observation that men do not live by bread alone. Nor does it offer much guidance for the 157 billion people, who, 35 years later (for Clark presumably finds something wicked in changing the present rate of growth), would number 314 billion. Clark's attitude is preecological (and the antithesis of what our book has taught): "'Better fifty years of Europe than a cycle of Cathay,'" he quotes approvingly from Tennyson.

John Maddox's *The Doomsday Syndrome* we consider the simplistic assurance that if we do enough of what we are doing we are sure to win. It is shallow in its understanding of ecology and is dedicated to the proposition that science is only a shadow of its hardware.

We have little to quarrel with in regard to *The Limits to Growth* (Dennis L. Meadows et al.) and *A Blueprint for Survival* (Goldsmith et al.). However, especially in regard to the former, we are concerned with a true decentralization so that individual wisdom can both be gained and made to count for something. Mere stabilization of population and economies seems secondary, although certainly necessary.

The Stockholm Conference has represented precisely the strategy that will not work. Its title, "The Human Environment," was hopelessly arrogant and unecological. Its spokesmen were almost entirely promoters of the highly centralized, dehumanized institutions that will never be capable of either using or generating ecological responsibility. The only kind of wisdom (almost unbelievably absent among bureaucrats) that will save us, if any will, is that of ecosystemically perceptive people who use hearts as well as heads—and who, since all the wisdom is not yet in, look to the ecosystem for cues as to what to do next. Integrity can be attained only if we are prepared to recognize integrity in ecosystemic nature and only if we can come to live in a way where every interaction is worthwhile. The bureaucratic manifestation of mind is simply not trustworthy.

Psychologist-anthropologist Gregory Bateson has put our dilemma aptly. In his Korzybski lecture (*General Semantics Bulletin* no. 37, 1970), he notes the immanence of what we think of as individual mind in the whole communication of the body within; and, as importantly, he finds mind equally "immanent in the total interconnected social system and planetary ecology." He rightly fears arrogance that sees the world around us as mindless and outside moral consideration, especially when that arrogance commands an advanced technology. Our disturbances are self-amplifying and, unless we take action, Earth will be torn apart. For that reason, learning to think fully about consequences of our actions is a habit of thought we have to acquire. "I suggest to you," he warns, "that we should trust no policy decisions which emanate from persons who do not yet have that habit."

It is difficult to know what Herman Mellville had in mind when he described the demise of the whaling ship *Pequod,* battered by Moby Dick, the great white whale. As the ship sank, it formed a great whirlpool that sucked down to their dooms all the crew except Ishmael. Ishmael was saved by the buoyant coffin of his friend Queequeg, a native of the wild islands of the South Seas. To us, part of Melville's message is that salvation lies in our capacity to grasp the unexpected truths generated by the uncultured other world of wild man and wilder nature.

Cities have previously been devastated by disease, and have survived. Can they survive what has been called "the last epidemic," that of their own violence? Furthermore, for all the dooms that have been visited upon individual cultures and communities in the past, man has never before come so near as now to exhausting the rich energy resources that he depends upon. Nor has there ever before been a time when the whole energy budget of the planet was endangered.

Compared to the minor patchwork miracles that we perform on sick people and, occasionally, on sick cities, the job ahead is formidable. The fact that our troubles are man-made may give us some hope that they can be man-cured. But we must give up any notion that Progress as we think of it is in any way related to true progress. True progress is possible only as an ecosystemic process.

Our Progress has proved destructive and delusive. Our chief failing has been that we have not thought of progress as related to the good of the whole ecosystem. Not only have our efforts to guide events been, in contrast to evolution with its vast resources of time, short-term; they have also been unfeeling, selfish, and loud. We have not been the responsible biotic citizens that we must, somehow, become.

Additional Help: Books and Other References

No effort has been made to provide a complete list of useful books that are currently available. Short articles and pamphlets have also been pretty much ignored, with a few exceptions and except for particularly pertinent contributions that are readily available in some of the anthologies and symposia listed in the general list (immediately below). Two useful compilations of references to environmental literature (and there are many others, including some comprehensive and specialized ones) are: John A. Moore, *Science for Society,* revised edition of an inexpensive publication of the American Association for the Advancement of Science, Washington, D.C., 1971; and Jack J. Bulloff, *Environmental Forum: Bibliography and Index to Environmental Literature through 1970* (books only), Science and Technology Studies, State University of New York at Albany, 1972.

Current literature is hard to keep up with and is greatly

dispersed. One of the most ambitious attempts to list all of it is *Environmental Information Access* and its annual index *The Environmental Index* ($150 and $50 per year, respectively, from Microfiche Systems Co., 305 East 46th Street, New York 10017).

Conservation organizations of various kinds may also have information available. The composition has changed somewhat but a valuable list of such organizations may be found in *Ecotactics: The Sierra Club Handbook for Environment Activists* (New York: Pocket Books, 1970).

GENERAL TITLES AND ANTHOLOGIES

Dorst, Jean. *Before Nature Dies* (Boston: Houghton Mifflin, 1970). One of the best accounts of nature conservation; it clearly shows how man has interacted with the rest of nature to produce the results we see.

Ehrlich, Paul R., and Anne H. Ehrlich. *Population, Resources, Environment: Issues in Human Ecology,* 2d ed. (San Francisco: Freeman, 1972). A fine book with extremely good lists of references at the ends of chapters; the subtitle indicates the breadth of coverage.

Ehrlich, Paul R., A. H. Ehrlich and J. P. Holdren. *Human Ecology: Problems and Solutions* (San Francisco: Freeman, 1973). A shortened version of the big book.

Farvar, M. Taghi, and J. P. Milton (eds.). *The Careless Technology* (Garden City. N. Y.: Natural History Press, 1972). This many-faceted volume has rich bibliographies documenting each of the more than fifty studies reported; readings especially applicable to part 3, concerning the impacts of technological development upon health and the patterns of human disease, will be immediately obvious; but almost all aspects of the troubles, except population problems, resulting from international technological development are covered in authoritative and refreshing detail.

Harte, John, and R. H. Socolow (eds.). *Patient Earth* (New York: Holt, paperback, 1971). Original papers by famous authors on soil conservation, resources, abortion, DDT, herbicides, wilderness, population control, the economics of stability, and physical constraints to growth.

Holdren, John P., and P. R. Ehrlich (eds.). *Global Ecology: Readings toward a Rational Strategy for Man* (New York: Harcourt Brace, paperback, 1971). Good articles from literature on resources, critical dangers, threatened species and legal, economic, demographic, and philosophical facets of the pickle we are in and how we might—and why we have to try to—get out.

Joffe, Joyce. *Conservation* (Garden City, N. Y.: Natural History Press, 1970). Part of a series—see books by Lauwerys and W. M. S. Russell in other sections—that is beautifully illustrated and considerably above the quality of most "conservation" books.

Johnson, Cecil E. (ed.). *Human Biology* (New York: Van Nostrand, paperback, 1970). An anthology of interesting materials by a concerned biologist.

Johnson, Huey D. (ed.). *No Deposit—No Return: Man and His Environment* (Reading, Mass.: Addison-Wesley, paperback, 1970). Original essays from a meeting in Earth Year One.

Kucera, Clair L. *The Challenge of Ecology* (St. Louis: C. V. Mosby Co., 1973). A sound ecology of processes in nature that affect man's dominant role in the world. The relevance of good ecological knowledge has rarely been made more evident.

Leinwand, Gerald (general ed.). *Problems of American Society* (New York: Washington Square, 1970). Separate paperbacks entitled: *The City as a Community; The Slums; The Traffic Jam; Air and Water Pollution; Crime and Juvenile Delinquency; The Draft; The Negro in the City; The Consumer; Poverty and the Poor; Civil Rights and Civil Liberties.*

Marsh, George Perkins. *The Earth as Modified by Human Action. A New Edition of Man and Nature.* Various editions of this are now available, including a facsimile reprint by Arno and the *New York Times,* 1970; a great, neglected classic.

McNaughton, S. J., and L. L. Wolf. *General Ecology* (New York: Holt, Rinehart, Winston, 1973). Good general ecology with admirable chapter on population and resources.

Rienow, Robert, and Leona Train Rienow. *Moment in the Sun* (New York: Ballantine, paperback, 1967). The senior author is a professor of political science and public affairs; the book is especially recommended for nonscientists who think there is no environmental problem.

Shepard, Paul, and Daniel McKinley (eds.). *The Subversive Science: Essays toward an Ecology of Man* (Boston: Houghton Mifflin, paperback, 1969). Extensive reading lists; some articles are cited separately below.

———, and ——— (eds.). *Environ/Mental: Essays on the Planet As a Home* (Boston: Houghton Mifflin, paperback, 1971). Reading lists; some papers are listed below.

Thomas, William L., Jr., (ed.). *Man's Role in Changing the Face of the Earth,* 2 volumes (Chicago: University of Chicago Press, paperback, 1956). Certainly the greatest meeting of scholarly minds up to its day and a useful starting point for modern students of human ecology.

Vayda, Andrew P. (ed.) *Environment and Cultural Behavior* (Garden City, N. Y.: Natural History Press, paperback, 1969). Many papers, most of them soundly based in ecological thinking.

Weisz, Paul B., (ed.). *The Contemporary Scene* (New York: McGraw-Hill, paperback, 1970). A well-informed look at man as a biological being in a complex world.

PART 1 DEFINITIONS AND PERSPECTIVES

Bates, Marston. *The Forest and the Sea* (New York: New American Library, paperback, 1961). An excellent and classic ecology text.

Darling, F. Fraser. "The Unity of Ecology," *Advancement of Science,* vol. 20, pp. 297–306, 1963. Reprinted in Shepard and McKinley, *Environ/Mental,* cited above in General Titles.

Dasmann, Raymond F. *Environmental Conservation,* 3d ed. (New York: Wiley, paperback, 1972). A balanced look at Earth as ecosystems that must be treated with full knowledge for reliable results.

Hardin, Garrett. *Nature and Man's Fate* (New York: Mentor, paperback, 1959). The relevance of biology to man is outlined in a book written well before public discovery of "environment."

Henderson, Leon J. *The Fitness of the Environment* (Boston: Beacon, paperback, 1958). First published 1913, this book provides good background for thought about the original fitness of Earth as human habitat and habitat where life could evolve.

Hocking, Brian. *Biology—or Oblivion: Lessons from the Ultimate Science* (Cambridge, Mass.: Schenkman, paperback, 1965). A sparkling introduction to what biology ought to be about.

Holling, C. S., and Gordon Orians. "Toward an Urban Ecology." *Bulletin, Ecological Society of America,* vol. 52, no. 2, pp. 2–6, June 1971.

Kormondy, Edward J. *Concepts of Ecology* (Englewood Cliffs, N. J.: Prentice-Hall, paperback, 1969). The most useful of the general ecology texts.

Odum, Eugene P. "The Strategy of Ecosystem Development," *Science,* vol. 164, pp. 262–270, 1969. Reprinted in Shepard and McKinley,

Environ/Mental cited above in General Titles. Odum is also the author of a most respected advanced ecology text.

Rudd, Robert L. *Pesticides and the Living Landscape* (Madison, Wis.: University of Wisconsin Press, paperback, 1964.) An excellent introduction by a biologist to the ecology of pest control and its failures.

Sears, Paul B. "The Inexorable Problem of Space," *Science,* no. 127, pp. 9–16, 1958. Reprinted in Shepard and McKinley, *The Subversive Science,* cited above in General Titles. Sears, a great pioneer in American conservation, is also author of many books, including *Deserts on the March* and *Where There Is Life.*

Watt, Kenneth E. F. *Principles of Environmental Science* (New York: McGraw-Hill, 1973.) This book contains fundamentally important chapters on ecological principles, ecological variables, weather, fossil fuels, appropriate strategies for various ecosystems, biological control in pest and disease management, epidemic aspects of human diseases, urban planning.

Woodwell, George M., et al. "A-bombs, Bugbombs, and Us," Brookhaven National Laboratory Publication no. 9842, 1966. Reprinted in Shepard and McKinley, *The Subversive Science,* cited above in General Titles.

PART 2 THE GATHERING OF THE CLAN

Adams, Robert M., and H. J. Nisson. *The Uruk Countryside; the Natural Setting of Urban Societies* (Chicago: University of Chicago Press, 1972).

Anderson, Edgar. *Plants, Man and Life* (Berkeley, Calif.: University of California Press, paperback, 1967.) A useful and interesting look at domestication; see also Ucko and Dimbleby, cited below.

Clark, Grahame. *The Stone Age Hunters* (New York: McGraw-Hill, paperback, 1967). A good look at modern primitives and an account of prehistory that is steeped in ecological thinking, as all Clark's works are; see also Lee and DeVore, cited below.

Darling, F. Fraser. *Wilderness and Plenty* (Boston: Houghton Mifflin, 1970). Beautifully written account of the ecological binds we are in, in historical context. He also has two good articles with important historical perspectives in the Shepard and McKinley anthologies cited above in General Titles.

Detwyler, Thomas R., and Melvin G. Marcus. *Urbanization and En-*

vironment: the Physical Geography of the City, (North Scituate, Mass.: Duxbury, paperback, 1972).

Halprin, Lawrence. *Cities* (New York: Reinhold, 1963). The views of a sensitive landscape architect and regional planner.

Harris, David R. "The Origins of Agriculture in the Tropics," *American Scientist,* vol. 60, pp. 180–193, 1972. Harris also has a good article in Ucko and Dimbleby.

Korzybski, Alfred. "Some Non-Aristotelian Data on Efficiency for Human Adjustment," *Second Amer. Congr. Gen. Semantics,* pp. 541–548, 1943.

Lauwerys, J. A. *Man's Impact on Nature* (Garden City, N. Y.: Natural History Press, 1970). Plain-spoken, well-written, and informed.

Lee, Richard B., and Irven DeVore (eds.). *Man the Hunter* (Chicago: Aldine, 1968). Offers fresh insights into a subject that has been badly interpreted in most conventional anthropological and economic thinking; see also books in this section by G. Clark and M. Sahlins and a pertinent paper by James V. Neel, "Lessons from a 'Primitive' People," *Science,* vol. 170, pp. 815–822, 1970.

Mellaart, James. "A Neolithic City in Turkey," *Scientific American.* vol. 210, no. 4, pp. 94–104, April, 1964. See also his book *Çatal Hüyük* (London: Heineman, 1968).

Milgram, Stanley. "The Experience of Living in Cities," *Science,* vol. 167, pp. 1461–1468, 1970. Reprinted in Shepard and McKinley, *Environ/Mental,* pp. 183–202, cited in General Titles.

Moholy-Nagy, Sibyl. *Matrix for Man* (New York: Praeger, 1969). An illustrated history of city patterns.

Mumford, Lewis. *The City in History* (New York: Harcourt, Brace, paperback, 1961). Well known and readable history.

Russell, W. M. S. *Man, Nature and History* (Garden City, N. Y.: Natural History Press, 1970).

Sahlins, Marshall. *Stone Age Economics* (Chicago: Aldine, 1972).

Sauer, Carl O. "Theme of Plant and Animal Destruction in Economic History," *Journal of Farm Economics,* vol. 20, pp. 765–775, 1938. Reprinted in Shepard and McKinley, *Environ/Mental,* cited above in General Titles. This is a classic study of effects of relatively early urban peoples upon environments of the Old and New Worlds.

Shepard, Paul. *Man in the Landscape: A Historic View of the Esthetics of Nature* (New York: Ballantine, paperback, 1967).

Ucko, Peter J., and G. W. Dimbleby (eds.). *The Domestication and Exploitation of Plants and Animals* (Chicago: Aldine, 1969). Contains copiously documented papers on early agriculture, domestication, and urbanism; the ecology of early domestication is especially well treated.

PART 3 THE POTTER AND THE POT

Ahmed, A. K., et al. "Control for Asbestos," *Environment*, vol. 14, no. 10, pp. 16–22, 27–29, December, 1972.

Barkley, Paul W., and D. W. Seckler. *Economic Growth and Environmental Decay: The Solution Becomes the Problem* (New York: Harcourt Brace, paperback, 1972).

Brodine, Virginia. *Air Pollution* (New York: Harcourt, Brace, Jovanovich, 1973).

Buel, Ronald A. *Dead End* (Penguin, p. 61, 1972).

Burnet, Macfarlane, and D. O. White. *Natural History of Infectious Diseases*, 4th ed. (New York: Cambridge University Press, paperback, 1972).

Carefoot, G. L., and E. R. Sprott. *Famine on the Wind* (Chicago: Rand McNally, 1967). Good popular account of plant diseases.

Carson, Rachel. *Silent Spring* (Boston: Houghton Mifflin, 1962). See also Robert Rudd, 1964. Frank Graham, Jr., has brought some of the issues up to date in his *Since Silent Spring* (Boston: Houghton Mifflin, 1970). Note also K. E. F. Watt, 1973, cited in Part 1.

Curtis, Richard, and Elizabeth Hogan. *Perils of the Peaceful Atom* (Garden City, N. Y.: Natural History Press, 1970). Strictures on one of the most popular "ways out."

Detwyler, Thomas R., and M. G. Marcus. *Urbanization and Environment: The Physical Geography of the City* (North Scituate, Mass.: Duxbury, 1972).

Dubos, René. *So Human an Animal* (New York: Scribner, paperback, 1969).

Edberg, Rolf. *On the Shred of a Cloud* (University, Ala.: University of Alabama Press, paperback, 1969). Beautifully written plea for international peace, with welcome overtones of ecological understanding.

Energy and Power. (San Francisco: Freeman, paperback, 1971). Notable chapters by Woodwell, Hutchinson and others on energy resources, cycles, uses, and elaborations.)

Farvar, Boyouk. "Biological Disorders of the Genito-urinary System Following the Introduction of New Technologies and Lifeways in the Less Developed Countries," in Farvar and Milton (eds.) *The Careless Technology* (Garden City, N. Y.: Natural History Press, 1972).

George, Carl J. "The Role of the Aswan High Dam in Changing the Fisheries of the Southeastern Mediterranean." See in Farvar and Milton, cited above in Farvar, Boyouk.

Georgescu-Roegen, Nicholas. *The Entropy Law and the Economic Process* (Cambridge, Mass.: Harvard University Press, 1971). A brief, lucid summary of this important and ecologically wise book has been published as "The Entropy Law and the Economic Problem," University of Alabama, Department of Economics, Distinguished Lecture Series no. 1, 1971.

Halprin, Lawrence. *New York, New York: A Study of the Quality, Character, and Meaning of Open Space in Urban Design.* Prepared for the City of New York by Lawrence Halprin and Associates, San Francisco, 1968.

Landsberg, Hans H., L. L. Fischman, and J. L. Fisher. *Resources in America's Future* (Baltimore: Johns Hopkins Press, 1963). A primary source of statistics; see also W. W. Murdoch, below.

Landsberg, Helmut E. *Weather and Health.* (Garden City, N. Y.: Doubleday Anchor, paperback, 1969). Landsberg is the author of some notable studies on the climates of cities. See also W. L. Thomas, *Man's Role in Changing the Face of the Earth,* cited above under General Titles, and a useful recent summary in "Man-made Climatic Changes," *Science,* vol. 170, pp. 1265–1274, 1970. See also the extensive bibliography in James T. Peterson, cited below, and the pertinent chapter in K. E. F. Watt, *Principles of Environmental Science,* cited in Part 1.

Lynch, Kevin. "The City as Environment," *Scientific American,* vol. 213, no. 3, pp. 209–219, September, 1965. One of a series of articles on the urban theme in that issue.

Michelson, William H. *Man and His Urban Environment: A Sociological Approach* (Reading, Mass.: Addison-Wesley, paperback, 1970). Good modern digest of current and historical views; bibliography.

Montagu, M. F. A. (ed.). *Culture* (New York: Oxford University Press, 1968). See R. Kuttner, "Cultural Selection of Human Psychological Types;" additional information in "The Silent Millenia in the Origin of Agriculture," in Ucko and Dimbleby, cited in Part 2.

Murdoch, William W. (ed.). *Environment: Resources, Pollution and Society* (Stamford, Conn.: Sinauer, paperback, 1971.) Well-documented and detailed summaries of statistics on world population, food production, and other aspects of resources; considers the varieties of pollution and legal implementation of ameliorative actions; excellent original papers.

Notkins, A. L., and H. Koprowski. "How the Immune Response to a Virus can cause disease," *Scientific American,* vol. 228, no. 1, pp. 22–31, January 1973.

Peterson, James T. "The Climate of Cities: A Survey of Recent Literature," U. S. National Air Pollution Control Administration Publication no. AP-59, 1969.

Pimentel, David, et al. "Food Production and the Energy Crisis," *Science,* vol. 182, pp. 443–449, 1973.

Rodda, Michael. *Noise and Society* (New York: Benjamin, paperback, 1967).

Shurcliff, William A. *S/S/T and Sonic Boom Handbook,* 2d ed. (New York: Ballantine, paperback, 1972).

Simmel, Georg. "The Metropolis and Mental Life," in Hatt and Reiss, *Cities and Society,* rev. ed. (New York: Free Press of Glencoe, 1957, pp. 635–646).

United Nations. *Chemical and Bacteriological (Biological) Weapons and the Effects of Their Possible Use* (New York: Ballantine, paperback, 1970).

U.S. Council on Environmental Quality. *Environmental Quality,* Annual Reports 1, 2, and 3, U.S. Government Printing Office, Washington, D.C., 1970, 1971, 1972.

Whiteside, Thomas. *Defoliation: What Are Our Herbicides Doing to Us?* (New York: Ballantine, paperback, 1970).

Wirth, Louis. "Urbanism As a Way of Life," *American Journal of Sociology,* vol. 44, pp. 1–24, 1938.

PART 4 WHY CITIES GROW GRAY

Audy, J. Ralph. "Measurement and Diagnosis of Health," in Shepard and McKinley, *Environ/Mental,* pp. 140–162, cited above in General Titles. Definitions of health and wise comments on how we make ourselves sick.

Bell, Gwen, and Jacqueline Tyrwhitt, eds. *Human Identity in the Urban Environment* (Baltimore: Penguin, 1972).

Bell, Gwen, et al. *Urban Environments and Human Behavior. An Annotated Bibliography* (Stroudsburg, Pa.: Dowden, Hutchinson & Ross, 1973).

Borgstrom, Georg. *Too Many: A Study of Earth's Biological Limitations* (New York: Macmillan, 1969). Detailed account of why our best efforts in providing food for world populations may not succeed.

Calhoun, John B. "The Ecology and Sociology of the Norway Rat," U.S. Public Health Service Publication no. 1008. See also "Population Density and Social Pathology," *Scientific American*, vol. 206, no. 2, pp. 139–148, February, 1962.

———. "Psycho-ecological Aspects of Population," in Shepard and McKinley, *Environ/Mental*, pp. 111–133, cited above in General Titles.

Clawson, Marion. *Surburban Land Conversion in the United States* (Baltimore: Johns Hopkins Press, 1971).

———. *America's Land and Its Uses* (Baltimore: Johns Hopkins Press, 1972).

Driver, Peter M. "Toward an ethology of human conflict: a review," *Journal of Conflict Resolution*, vol. 11, pp. 361–374, 1967.

Elddredge, H. Wentworth (ed.) *Taming Megalopolis*, 2 vols. (Garden City, N.Y.: Doubleday, 1967).

Greenbie, Barrie B. "What can we learn from other animals? Behavioral biology and the ecology of cities," *American Institute of Planners (AIP) Journal*, vol. 37, pp. 162–168, 1971.

———. "Science and the Planners: A Tale of Two Worlds; Group Territory and Social Space," *Man-Environment Systems*, vol. 2, pp. 179–181 and 365–369, 1972.

Halprin, Lawrence. *Freeways* (New York: Reinhold, 1966).

Hardin, Garrett. *Birth Control* (New York: Pegasus, paperback, 1970).

Hutt, S. J. and Corinne Hutt, (eds.) *Early Human Development* (New York: Oxford University Press, 1973).

Jacobs, Jane. *The Death and Life of Great American Cities* (New York: Random House, 1961).

Kyllonen, R. L., "Crime Rate *vs.* Population Density in United States Cities: a Model." *General Systems*, vol. 12, pp. 137–145, 1967.

Leyhausen, Paul. "The Sane Community—A Density Problem?", *Discovery*, vol. 26, pp. 27–33, 1965. Reprinted in Shepard and McKinley, *Environ/Mental*, cited above in General Titles.

Linton, Ron M. *Terracide* (Boston: Little, Brown, 1970).

Lorenz, Konrad, and Paul Leyhausen. *Motivation of Human and Animals Behavior.* (Cincinnati: Van Nostrand Reinhold, 1973).

Meyer, Jon K. "Bibliography on the Urban Crisis: The Behavioral, Psychological, and Sociological Aspects of the Urban Crisis," U.S.

Public Health Service Publication no. 1948, 1969. Contains Cross-indexed references to nearly 2,800 publications.

Mishan, Ezra J. *Technology and Growth: The Price We Pay* (New York: Praeger, 1970). Splendid analysis by an economist; the automobile, as an example of what we are doing to ourselves, comes off as a decided danger.

The President's Commission on Population Growth and the American Future. *Population and the American Future,* U.S. Government Printing Office, Washington, 1972. An excellent digest of the facts on various patterns and trends of growth and their likely results; must reading for everybody.

Schmid, A. Allan. *Converting Land from Rural to Urban Uses* (Baltimore: Johns Hopkins Press, paperback, 1968).

Srole, Leo, et al. *Mental Health in the Metropolis: The Midtown Manhattan Study,* New York: Blakiston, McGraw-Hill, 1962).

Tinbergen, N. "On war and peace in animals and man," *Science,* vol. 160, pp. 1411–1418, 1968.

———. "Functional ethology and the human sciences," *Royal Society of London, Proceedings,* B, vol. 182, pp. 385–410, 1972.

PART 5 CURING MISEDUCATION

Ayres, Robert U., and A. V. Kneese. "Economic and Ecological Effects of a Stationary Economy," *Annual Review of Ecology and Systematics,* vol. 2, pp. 1–22, 1971.

Bateson, Gregory. *Steps to an Ecology of Mind* (New York: Ballantine, paperback, 1972). A good introduction to what constitutes ecologically pathological thinking and to the value of both skin-in and skin-out ecologies.

Caldwell, Lynton K. *Environment: A Challenge for Modern Society* (Garden City, N.Y.: Natural History Press, 1970).

Caldwell, Lynton K. *In Defense of Earth: International Protection of the Biosphere* (Bloomington, Ind.: Indiana University Press, 1972).

Clark, Colin. *Population Growth and Land Use* (New York: St. Martin's Press, 1967). A fair summary of Clark's views appear in his essay "Agricultural Productivity in Relation to Population," in Gordon Wolstenholm (ed.), *Man and His Future,* pp. 23–35, Ciba Foundation, London: J. and A. Churchill, 1963. Nobody seems to have examined fully most of Clark's ecologically relevant statements but some of his demographic shortcomings are challenged by population expert Kingsley Davis in "Colin Clark and the Benefits of an Increase in Population," *Scientific American,* vol. 218, no. 4, pp. 133–138, April, 1968.

Cobb, Edith. "The Ecology of Imagination in Childhood," in Shepard and McKinley, *The Subversive Science,* cited above in General Titles.

Collier, John. "Fullness of Life through Leisure," in Shepard and McKinley, *The Subversive Science,* cited above in General Titles.

Daly, Herman E. "The Stationary-State Economy: Toward a Political Economy of Biophysical Equilibrium and Moral Growth," University of Alabama, Department of Economics, Distinguished Lecture Series no. 2. See also Daly's chapter on steady-state economy in Harte and Socolow, *Patient Earth,* cited above in General Titles.

——— (ed.). *Toward a Steady-State Economy,* (San Francisco: Freeman, 1973).

Darling, F. Fraser. *West Highland Survey: An Essay in Human Ecology* (New York: Oxford University Press, 1955). A perceptive modern study that is one of the few real ecologies of man.

——— and J. P. Milton (eds.). *Future Environments of North America* (Garden City, N.Y.: Natural History Press, 1966). A mixture of viewpoints; original papers.

Dasmann, Raymond F. *A Different Kind of Country.* New York: Macmillan, 1968.

Dorney, R. S. 1973. "Role of ecologists as consultants in urban planning and design," *Human Ecology,* vol. 1, pp. 183–200, 1973.

Egler, Frank E. *The Way of Science: A Philosophy of Ecology for the Layman,* (New York: Hafner, 1970). Uncompromisingly sane viewpoints of a practitioner of the art.

Elton, Charles S. *The Ecology of Invasions by Animals and Plants* (London: Methuen, 1958). Good ecology, from a perspective that has been neglected; two noteworthy final chapters on conservation philosophy are highlights.

Falk, Richard A. *This Endangered Planet.* (New York: Random House, 1971).

Fegely, Thomas, et al. *Recycling. An Interdisciplinary Approach to Environmental Education* (Emmaus, Pa.: Rodale Press, Organic Classroom Series no. 2, 1973.)

Fuller, R. Buckminster. *Utopia or Oblivion* (New York: Bantam Books, paperback, 1969).

Glikson, A. *The Ecological Basis of Planning* (The Hague: Martinus Nijhof, 1971). A European view, well informed and searching.

Goldsmith, Edward, et al. *Blueprint for Survival. By the Editors of The Ecologist* (Boston: Houghton Mifflin, 1972).

Halprin, Lawrence. *The RSVP Cycles: Creative Processes in the Human Environment,* (New York: Braziller, 1969).

Hardin, Garrett. *Exploring New Ethics for Survival* (New York: Viking, 1972). Provocative enlargement of his famous "Tragedy of the Commons," an enquiry into why what belongs to everybody is protected by nobody—and what can be done about it.

Heller, Alfred, ed. 1972. *The California Tomorrow Plan,* rev. ed. William Kaufman, Los Altos (paperback).

Illich, Ivan. *Celebration of Awareness: A Call for Institutional Revolution* (Garden City, N. Y.: Doubleday, 1970). One chapter is his penetrating essay "Outwitting the 'Developed' Countries," which is reprinted in Holdren and Ehrlich, *Global Ecology,* cited above in General Titles.

———. *Deschooling Society* (New York: Harper and Row, 1970).

Leopold, Aldo. *A Sand County Almanac* (New York: Oxford University Press, 1949).

McHarg, Ian L. *Design with Nature* (Garden City, N. Y.: Natural History Press, 1969). Magnificently illustrated interpretation of ecology for man.

McKinley, Daniel. "Earth *and* Myth—or Earth *versus* Myth?" *Forum for Correspondence and Contact,* vol. 5, no. 1, pp. 135–140, May 1973.

"Man and Nature in the City," U. S. Bureau of Sport Fisheries and Wildlife, Washington, D. C., 1969.

Meadows, D. H. et al. *The Limits to Growth.* (New York: Universe Books, 1972).

Murphy, Earl Finbar. *Man and His Environment: Law* (New York: Harper and Row, paperback, 1971).

Odum, Howard T. *Environment, Power, and Society* (New York: Wiley-Interscience, paperback, 1971). A modern, socially relevant look at human ecology by a systems ecologist and field biologist.

The President's Science Advisory Committee. *Restoring the Quality of Our Environment,* Report of the Environmental Pollution Panel, The White House, Washington, D. C., 1965.

Rowat, Donald C., (ed.). *The Ombudsman: Citizen's Defender* (Toronto: University of Toronto Press, 1965).

Sanders, Norman K. *Stop It! A Guide to Defense of the Environment*

(San Francisco: Rinehart, paperback, 1972). Both legal and citizen-action avenues are discussed.

Sax, Joseph L. *Defending the Environment: A Strategy for Citizen Action* (New York: Knopf, 1971).

Shomon, Joseph James. *Open Land for Urban America* (Baltimore: Johns Hopkins Press, 1971). Many practical examples of what can be done.

"Soil, Water and Suburbia," U. S. Departments of Agriculture and Housing and Urban Development, U. S. Government Printing Office, Washington, 1968.

Starr, Robert. *Urban Choices: The City and Its Critics* (New York: Coward-McCann, 1967).

Index

Index